Soap Carving Ocean and Coral Reef Creatures

Howard K. Suzuki

Schiffer Publishing Ltd

4880 Lower Valley Road Atglen, Pennsylvania 19310

Dedication

I want to dedicate this book to Tets, Georganne, Pierre, and Ted without whom this book would not have been completed.

Other Schiffer Books by Howard K. Suzuki

Other Schiffer Books on Related Subjects
The Carver's Book of Aquatic Animals,
0-88740-734-X, $39.95
Carving in Soap: North American Animals,
0-7643-1292-8, $12.95
Soap Carving for Children of All Ages,
0-7643-0859-9, $12.95

Copyright © 2007 by Howard K. Suzuki
Library of Congress Control Number: 2007929265

Designed by Mark David Bowyer
Type set in Elphinstone™ / Korinna BT

ISBN: 978-0-7643-2754-4
Printed in China

Published by Schiffer Publishing Ltd.
4880 Lower Valley Road
Atglen, PA 19310
Phone: (610) 593-1777; Fax: (610) 593-2002
E-mail: Info@schifferbooks.com

For the largest selection of fine reference books on this and related subjects, please visit our web site at
www.schifferbooks.com
We are always looking for people to write books on new and related subjects. If you have an idea for a book please contact us at the above address.

This book may be purchased from the publisher.
Include $3.95 for shipping.
Please try your bookstore first.
You may write for a free catalog.

In Europe, Schiffer books are distributed by
Bushwood Books
6 Marksbury Ave.
Kew Gardens
Surrey TW9 4JF England
Phone: 44 (0) 20 8392-8585; Fax: 44 (0) 20 8392-9876
E-mail: info@bushwoodbooks.co.uk
Website: www.bushwoodbooks.co.uk
Free postage in the U.K., Europe; air mail at cost.

Acknowledgments

I want to thank Douglas Congdon-Martin, editor at Schiffer Publishing, for encouraging me to write my third soap-carving book. His confidence in my abilities is very much appreciated. Next, I want to thank Cindy Lott, my long time friend, marine biologist and scuba diving buddy for letting me use her underwater photographs of the seahorse and octopus. Finally, I want to thank my wife, Tetsuko, for her patience and understanding while I was writing and working on the book, and for her reading and editing of the manuscript. Without their support and help, this book would not have been conceived or written.

Table of Contents

Introduction

My first book about soap carving was titled *Soap Carving For Children of All Ages*. The main objective of the book was to introduce the reader, young and old, to the fun of soap carving using easily made simple carving tools. Secondly, it was my hope that the book would be useful in teaching children some basics of three-dimensional arts, and help improve their artistic and motor skills. Thirdly, it was, and still is, my strong belief that soap carving can be useful to elderly individuals and disabled patients to maintain and improve their upper extremity "activities of daily living" skills.

My second book, *Carving in Soap: North American Animals,* introduced the techniques of fusing multiple bars of Ivory® Soap, which expands the creative possibilities of soap bars as a carving medium

The intent of this book is to follow the basic tenets of my previous books and expand the creative possibilities of the use of bars of soap as a carving medium. The format of the book will begin with carving subjects using a single bar of soap, followed by subjects carved with different configurations of fused multiple bars of soap. Carvings will include in-the-round, shallow relief and deep relief and caricature styles. In addition, several different methods of mounting and displaying the carvings will be shown.

Each chapter lists basic or special techniques to be emphasized. This is followed by a short description of the biology of the animal. With the exception of the actual photographs of the seahorse and octopus, all other photographs were taken by the author. The patterns for the animals are reproduced at 100% the size of the Ivory Soap® bar.

The animals chosen for this book are well-known, popular animals. With the exceptions of the Orca and Manatee, the animals selected have not been described in my prior books. Also included are animals without backbones (invertebrates).

While this book only describes marine animals, it is my hope that you use this book to expand your own creative abilities and use it to design and carve subjects that are of particular interest to you. With this in mind, several blank soap bars templates are included in the last chapter. You can copy them and use them to draw your own patterns

Enjoy and have fun!

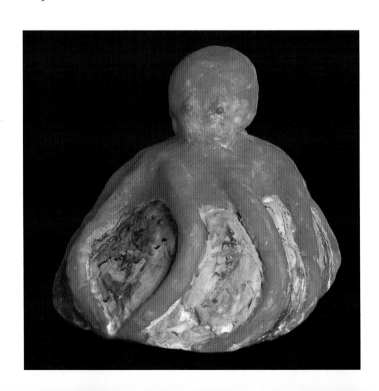

Chapter One
General Techniques

Ivory Soap®

Ivory Soap® is the primary carving medium used in this book. It is a rectangular shaped white bar with a firm, even consistency, superb for carving. In addition, it is relatively inexpensive and can be readily fused together to form different multi-bar shapes. The more expensive cosmetic soaps come in different shapes. This makes it difficult to transfer patterns on to them. In addition, they do not have the right consistency and as a result, it is more difficult to carve. Also some people may be allergic to the aromatic chemicals in those soaps.

Ivory Soap® bar

Metal tools

While wooden carving tools will be the main tools used in this book, I also like to use steel straight bladed carving knives to quickly scrape off the logo on the soap and to rough out the outlined pattern. The potato peeler and cheese cutter are also useful tools to use. The former can be used as a gouge. The cheese cutter is useful in getting into tight spaces to remove material. Scissors are essential to cut the outlines of the patterns. Measuring devices such as calipers and rulers are essential tools to have and use. I use the calipers to make sure that structures are located in the proper positions. There is nothing worse than to have cockeyed eyes on a carving. The calipers are also used to compare dimensions between the carving and the pattern to help determine how much more must be removed.

Metal knives: top, straight blade; middle, curved blade; bottom, Skew blade.

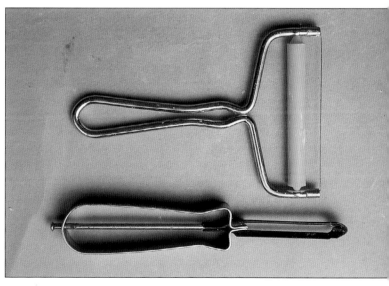

Top, cheese cutter; bottom, Apple-potato peeler.

Top: caliper. Middle: ruler. Bottom: scissors.

Wooden-carving tools

Wooden-carving tools such as chisels, skews, gouges, curved blade knives, and scrapers will be the main types of tools used in this book. They are easy and fun to make, and safe to use. My *Soap Carving for Children of All Ages* detailed the directions for making these wooden carving tools.

Angled blades like skews are useful to get into tighter areas. Gouges are useful in roughing out the carving and making concave cuts. Chisels are used to make straight cuts. The tools are made out of craft sticks available at various craft stores. They are also found as handles of frozen ice cream and colored frozen ice bars. After eating the frozen delights, save the sticks and make carving tools out of them. Small waste scraps of hardwoods can also be made into tools and scrapers.

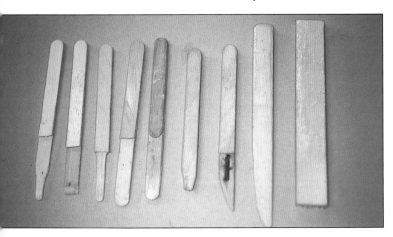

Wooden carving tools from left to right: 0.1875" wide chisel, 0.385" wide chisel, 0.1875" wide #0 gouge, 0.375" wide #0 gouge, 0.375" wide #3 gouge, 0.250" wide #10 gouge, skew blade, curved blade, and square cornered scraper.

Scribing tools

Scribers made out of wooden skewers and/or needles inserted in the end of wooden dowels are useful to outline patterns, to locate structural parts on a carving by punching holes through the pattern placed over the carvings, to make shallow grooves on fins to simulate digits on flippers, etc. A sewing needle can be inserted into the drilled end of a 0.375" diameter wooden dowel. Smaller scribers can be made using the common or silk pin and attaching them on a 0.125" diameter dowels. A shortened kabob barbeque skewer stick (0.125" in diameter) inserted into a drilled hole at the end of a 0.1875" diameter hardwood dowel makes an excellent wooden scriber. Pointed round wooden and plastic toothpicks (e.g., Forster® Party Sticks) also make good scribers. Both kabob skewers and round toothpicks are sold in grocery stores.

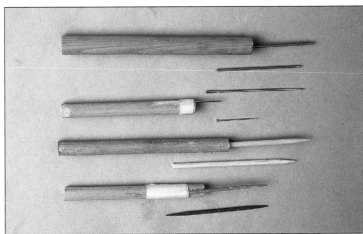

Scribing needles: top, Steel 0.0625" wire (or sewing needle) inserted into wooden dowel; second level, Kebob skewer inserted into dowel; third level, Common pin taped to dowel; bottom, Forster's Party Sticks® taped to dowel.

Plastic carving tools

Plastic spoons and knives for picnics and fast food restaurants can also be useful to make additional carving tools. Cutting off the terminal part of a spoon, and sharpening the cut straight edge will make a gouge.

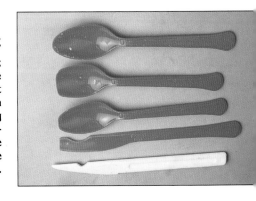

Plastic tools: top, Spoon; 0.625" wide #4 gouge; below, 0.5" wide #4 gouge; next level, red knife with concave scraping surface; bottom, white knife sharpened to have straight edge.

Some General Techniques

Scraping

In order to use Ivory Soap®, the logo must be scraped off. A scraper can be made out of scrap wood or aluminum plate measuring approximately 1.0" wide, 4.0" long and 0.125" thick with sharp 90 degrees angles on the long edges. Other scrapers can be made out of plastic knives, or straight bladed steel knives. The scraper is held at approximately a 70-80 degrees angle and moved across the surface to be scraped.

Scraping soap with straight square-edged wooden scraper: the scraper is used to remove the logo on the bar of soap and to flatten and smooth broad surfaces.

Transferring pattern

After the pattern has been copied, it may be glued on to a heavier backing such as cardboard, plastic, or index card paper. The outlines are cut to the approximate shape of the pattern, and placed on the soap bar. The pattern is then outlined on the soap with a scriber.

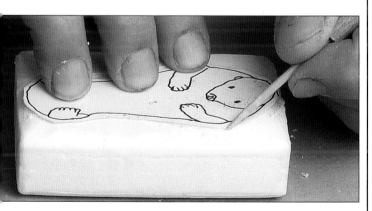

The scribing needle is used to transfer the pattern onto the soap-carving medium.

Initial roughing out

By placing the soap bar on a cutting surface, such as a ceramic tile, a straight bladed knife is oriented vertically on the outer edge of the soap and pushed down towards the tile. Do not attempt to cut too large a piece off of the soap as the bar may fragment and make the soap useless.

The soap can also be held by hand with the knife held at a right angle to the thickness of the bar. Continue carving until the outlined shape is attained. When using a steel knife, care must be taken not to cut oneself when moving the blade across the soap.

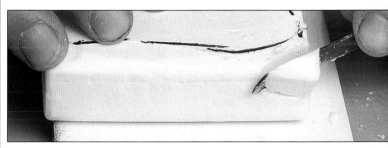

The soap bar is placed on a ceramic tile, and a long straight blade is used to rough out the outline of the pattern.

The pattern may also be roughed out by handholding the soap and carving with the other hand.

Removing debris

It is important to keep the carving area free of debris. The table should be cleaned frequently and soap and other debris removed. I use a wooden scraper to move the soap fragments and particles to the edge of the table and drop them in a large paper sack. Other than using some pieces to make the soap paste, I have not yet found a way to use this pile of good usable soap fragments. I do not think that I will resort to what my mother used to do. She placed the soap remnants into a small covered wire basket with a handle and swished the basket in a dishpan to form soapsuds to clean dishes.

Keep the carving areas clean by disposing soap debris into a large paper sack or waste container.

Maintaining clean and sharp tools

Carving tools should be cleaned frequently to remove the soap stuck on the blades. The stuck soap will impede clean cuts. It may be necessary to rinse the tools in running water occasionally. In addition, I frequently sharpen my carving tools on a sheet of fine sandpaper (150-220 grit).

Pictured is the act of sharpening a wooden-carving tool on sandpaper.

Soap Paste

Soap paste is a very important component of soap carving. It is used as glue and defect filler. It is made by placing soap debris moistened with water in a capped bottle. It is mixed with a flat-edged tool until an evenly consistent paste is formed. I prefer to use fresh paste, no more than a month old. If it is stored and not used for a long period it will turn yellow, even though it may still look like paste. Toothbrush and paper towels are useful in cleaning and removing waste debris.

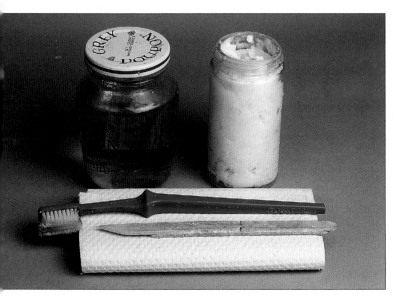

Top left: water bottle, soap paste in bottle. Front: toothbrush, spatula, and paper towel.

Fusing soap bars

Soap bars may be glued together in a number of different configurations. The fused soap bars can be used to create larger and more complex carvings or different shapes of bases. Several different designs of fused soap bars are used in this book. Only fresh bars of soap should be used, as old stored soap will dry, become brittle and is difficult to carve.

In order to glue soap together, the surfaces to be glued should have flat adjacent surfaces. Those surfaces are then placed on a dish holding a little bit of water, and the soap bars are allowed to soften. Soap paste is placed on the surfaces to be glued, and bars are pressed together and allowed to dry. In some instances, you can place wooden pins in the soap to be fused. This will strengthen the joints. After the two bars are pressed together, add soap paste into the joints in order to fill the cracks. It may be necessary to add several coatings of paste. As the soap paste hardens, it will shrink.

The glued parts are then stored in a Ziploc® plastic sealable bag. This will allow the surfaces to dry slowly and evenly. It usually takes a day or two for the soap to firm up and be ready for carving.

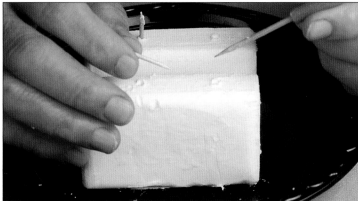

The long narrow edges of two Ivory Soap® bars are squared off using a scraper. Then those surfaces are softened in water. Ivory soap paste is added to the two edges, and two wooden pins are pushed into one of the bars to add stability to the bars.

The two soap bars are then pressed together. Slurry of soap paste is added to the joints as shown in the photograph. Allow to dry. Store the fused bar in a sealed Ziploc® bag.

Repairing breaks

Unfortunately, while carving soap, breaks will occur or worse yet the break takes place on a nearly completed soap carving. Not all of the breaks are the fault of the carver. Sometimes minor defects occur in the soap such as a slight difference in consistency of the soap. However, most of the breaks occur because the carver gets careless or tries to be too aggressive in carving. For your information, I do not exclude myself from this fault.

Soap paste can be applied to the moistened broken parts and held together. If there is enough carving material available, a short metal pin can be inserted to strengthen the joint. Hold it together while the paste hardens. After the paste has hardened you may need to add additional paste and let it dry. After drying the glued parts can be shaped, but care must be taken not to apply much pressure on the joint.

In the repair of delicate parts, such as the break of a fin or flipper, or if the break occurs after you have completed the carving, a more drastic measure may be necessary. Cyanoacrylate glues, such as Superglue® or Zap®, are excellent to join or coat completely shaped carved parts. Because cyanoacrylates dry much harder than the soap medium, it is not possible to do any further detailing without destroying or causing the repair area to break adjacent to the original location. **Care must also be used in applying superglue, as any contact with the skin will glue it together. The other cautionary note is that the fumes could be toxic.**

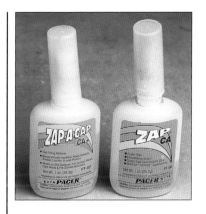

Cyanoacrylic glues: left, gap-filling Zap® glue; right: thin, penetrating Zap® glue.

Sanding, smoothing, and burnishing the carving

After the desired shape of the carving is reached, minor defects need to be removed. A small skew knife can be used as a scraper to even out some of the undesirable hills and valleys. This is then followed by gently rubbing 150-180 grit sandpaper or a medium grade non-woven abrasive pad (e.g. Scotch-Brite®) over the carving. The advantage of using the non-woven abrasive pad is that it can be renewed by rinsing the pad in water and dried. Finally the carving surfaces may be gently rubbed with a moistened plastic sponge. Care must be taken not to have the sponge too wet or to rub too vigorously or you could drastically alter the shape of your carving and weaken it.

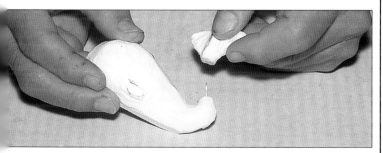

A broken part of the whale fluke showing a metal pin inserted into the caudal peduncle to strengthen the joint before it is glued with soap paste.

Burnishing accessories: top left, Scotch Brite® packing; bottom left, Scotch Brite® cut medium abrasive pad; top right, fine abrasive pad (different brand); middle Right, 150 grit wet and dry sandpaper; lower right, Cut plastic sponge.

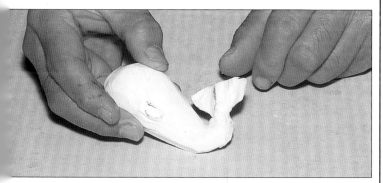

The fluke is now attached to the caudal peduncle of the whale and the carving is repaired.

Storing unfinished carvings

I always place an unfinished carving in a Ziploc® bag or equivalent. I then moisten a piece of folded paper towel and place it in the bag with the carving, which is then sealed. If you are not going to carve the piece for several days, it is best to check to see that the paper towel is still moist. If the carving dries out, the surface will become brittle and unworkable.

Storing soap carving in a sealable (e.g. Ziploc®) plastic bag.

Some Special Techniques

Making and inserting eyes

Eyes used in this book are of several types and are attached by pins. Dressmaker pins have small different colored round heads. Other pins have small, unpainted heads, like the silk pin. In order to use the latter pin, the head is dipped in enamel paint and inserted vertically into a plastic foam drying rack with its head down. Depending on the size of the painted head desired, one or more coats may be needed. For slightly larger eyes, glass beads inserted with silk pins can be used. Various wood-carving and taxidermy companies carry different sizes of wired glass eyes; however, an individual pair of eyes purchased from such companies is significantly higher in cost. **If you do not want to make or purchase eyes, you can always paint the eyes on your carving.**

Several tools are required for making simple eyes. Wire cutting pliers are used to cut the pins to their proper length. A hemostat or its equivalent, and/or forceps are used to hold the pins when either dipping the heads in the paint or inserting in the carving. Scribers, previously described, are used to mark the locations of the eye on the head.

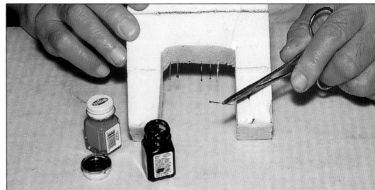

Eye storage and drying rack showing a pin dipped in black enamel ready to be placed upside down on the drying-storage rack.

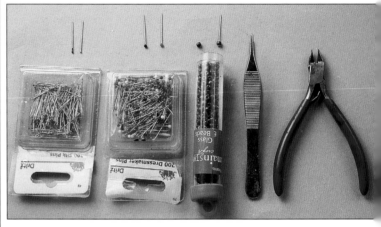

Eye making tools: from right to left; Side-cutting pliers fine forceps, glass beads with a bead attached to a silk pin, dressmaker's pins with round heads, and silk pins.

Adding vibrissae (chin hairs)

The insertion of "vibrissae" on the face of some sea mammals such as a the sea lion, walrus, seals and manatees adds significantly to the "wow" factor of a soap carving. The hairs are not difficult to insert but do require some delicate fine hand/eye coordination.

The most important factor in adding "vibrissae" is to find the right material that will serve as the hairs. My early vibrissae were bristles cut from an old boar's hair brush that I owned and used, as the bristles were stiff and quite suitable. However, it is not practical to recommend that one purchase an expensive brush just to get a few bristles for vibrissae on a carving.

I found that the "hairs" taken from inexpensive black disposable glue brushes purchased at hardware stores were the most suitable materials to make vibrissae. Since the fibers have varying diameters, the appropriate thicknesses of the "hairs" must be selected for each carving.

The only tools needed are a pair of scissors to cut the brush fibers, a fine pair of forceps, and a fine pin needle (scriber) attached to a handle. The stiffer hairs can be inserted directly into the soap with a pair of forceps. The finer hairs need to have fine holes poked into the carving and the hairs inserted into the holes. After insertion the hairs are cut to appropriate lengths.

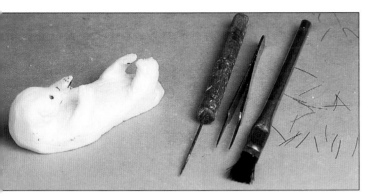

Tools for adding vibrissae: from left to right, needle scriber, fine forceps, and disposable glue brush. Note: the brush hairs are cut using a pair of scissors.

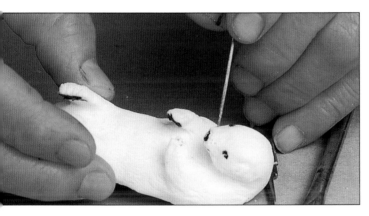

A fine needle is used to punch tiny holes in chin area for insertion of more delicate vibrissae. Stiffer vibrissae can be inserted directly into the chin area without making prior holes.

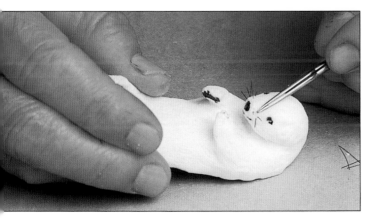

The vibrissae are inserted into the chin of a Sea Otter carving with a pair of fine forceps.

Mini-texturing brush

Commercially available small steel or brass brushes are too big and clumsy to use on soap carvings. I wanted a small brush with fibers extending on the plane of the handle. I found that the ordinary insulated braided copper wires used for 110-volt table lamps, etc were most suitable. All that was needed was 2.0" of one of the insulated braided copper wires. One end of the insulated wire was inserted into the end of a 0.1875" diameter dowel previously drilled with a hole to insert the wire and insulation. After insertion, about 0.50" of the terminal exposed end had the insulation removed and the braided wire exposed. The copper braids were opened forming the micro-wire brush.

Fur may be simulated by texturing the carving using the mini-brush. This will groove the carving to simulate fur. Its use is described in Chapter 4 on the Sea Otter.

Mini-brush for sculpturing "fur" on soap carvings: the left shows the exposed copper braided electrical wire; the right shows the completed mini-brush made by inserting the insulated part of the wire into a wooden dowel.

Optional Painting of carvings

Watercolors are the primary paints used in this book partially because they are available in relatively inexpensive sets and they are easy and safe to use. A dab of watercolor from a tube is placed on a multiple watercolor tray and water from an eyedropper is used to dilute the paint to the proper consistency. Different colors can be added to the different trays and the desired colors can be created. I am not an expert two-dimensional artist-painter so I like to keep things simple. I use only three brushes; one with a fine point and two medium point brushes. I keep one of the medium brushes as a dry brush to soften the effects of the colors. I keep a good supply of paper towels handy. The paper towels are too large for me to use, so I cut a roll of paper towel in half

with a saw. I feel that this is a more cost effective utilization of our resources. The only downside is that the rolls look like heavy-duty toilet paper!

The drying of the paints can be accelerated by using a hair dryer at low heat to blow warm air on the carving. Young children or disabled individuals may need to have help in using the hair dryer.

References

Suzuki, H.K. *Soap Carving for Children of All Ages*. Atglen, Pennsylvania: Schiffer Publishing, Ltd. 1999.

Suzuki, H.K. *Carving in Soap: North American Animals*. Atglen, Pennsylvania: Schiffer Publishing, Ltd. 2001.

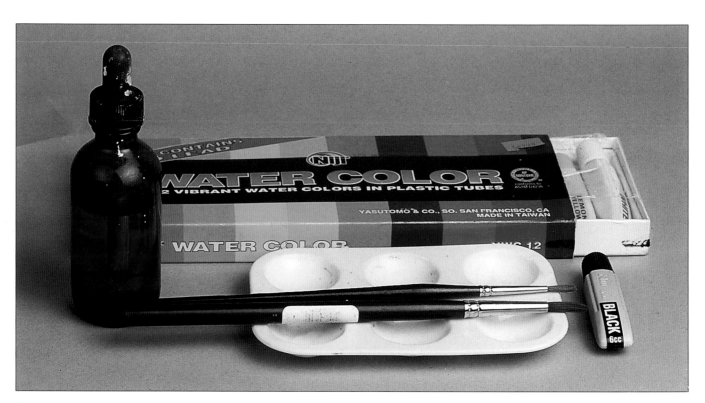

Painting supplies, which includes eye dropper, water bottle, paste, water color set, brushes and compartmentalized paint tray.

Chapter Two
Starfish

Basic techniques

1. Two carving patterns were designed based on the shape of a bar of Ivory Soap®
2. Basic carving techniques described for this initial carving

    A.   Preparing the soap bar by scraping off the Ivory Soap® logo
    B.   Keeping the carving area clean of soap debris
    C.   Using the carving tools to rough out and detail the carving
    D.   Burnishing or smoothing the carving
    E.   Painting the carving

The starfish belongs to a group of animals without a backbone (Invertebrates) called echinoderms (from the Latin *spiny skins)*. The group also includes the brittle star, sea urchin and sea cucumber. The starfishes are characterized by having radially symmetrical bodies with multiple arms ranging from five to many arms. They move along the bottom of the ocean using multiple tiny suckers on the bottom surface to help pull water through its undersurface, and thus slide over the bottom. The arms are flexible and envelope a prey with its multiple arms and suckers. The mouth is located in the center of the ventral surface of the body.

The starfish was selected as the initial carving for this book because it is a relatively simple animal to carve. Two designs are presented. The first pattern was based on a photograph of a starfish attached to a rugged rock. The shape of the starfish utilizes the entire rectangular shape of the Ivory Soap® bar. The second pattern is that of a symmetrically shaped five-armed starfish. Since only a portion of the soap bar is used in this pattern, the starfish will be smaller in size. The carving of the symmetrical starfish will be described.

References

Talbot, Frank and Roger Steene. *Reader's Digest Book of the Great Barrier Reef.* Sydney, Australia: Reader's Digest Services Pty Ltd., pp. 215-237, 1984.
Zeiller, Warren. *Tropical Marine Invertebrates of Southern Florida and the Bahamas Islands.* New York, NY: John Wiley and Sons, 1974.

Starfish, Papua New Guinea, South Pacific

Blue Starfish, Fiji Islands, South Pacific

Left, Starfish design using a full sized Ivory Soap® bar. Right, Starfish pattern using a squared off Ivory Soap® bar.

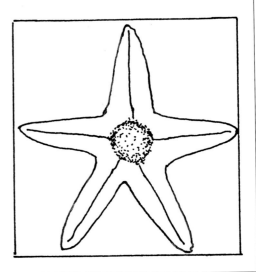

Scrape the Ivory Soap® logos off of both surfaces of the soap bar by moving a scraping tool across the surface at approximately 70 or 80 degree angles. Thin curled slices of soap will be removed. Review the discussion on scraping in Chapter One on General Techniques.

Keep the carving areas clean by frequently sweeping the soap debris into a waste container, such as a large paper bag.

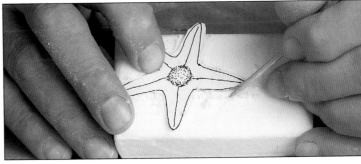

Place the starfish pattern on the bar and use a wooden needle to score the outline of the starfish.

Place the soap bar on a cutting board and make vertical cuts to square off the soap bar. Turn the bar over and make similar cuts. Repeat the process until the smaller segment breaks off. The starfish pattern is marked with a black Sharpie® pen so that the outline can be seen better; however, the use of the marking pen is optional.

Make vertical grooves following the outlines of the arms of the starfish using a skew blade knife. Those vertical grooves will serve as "stop gaps" for the next step.

Repeat making the horizontal cuts to the "stop gaps". Continue alternating between making vertical grooves and horizontal cuts until the starfish arms are outlined.

Orient the skew blade horizontally and carve the soap to remove the material to the depth of the grooves along the "stop gaps" outlining the starfish arms.

This shows the roughed out starfish.

Repeat making the vertical grooves outlining the arms. The part of the starfish carving adjacent to the right index finger shows how it should look after making the horizontal cuts.

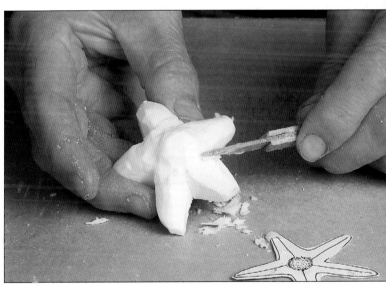

Shape the starfish arms by curving the arms slightly downward and rounding the upper surfaces. Carve a modified hemisphere in the center of the starfish to represent the round elevated dorsal part of the body.

Turn the starfish over on to its ventral side. Use a shallow gouge to carve the undersurfaces at the origins of the arms to form a concave shape. Leave a slight bulge for the central circular body.

Finish detailing the shapes of the arms and body by thinning and shaping the arms on both ventral and dorsal surfaces.

The carving is initially smoothed by scraping the carving with a skew blade as shown in the photograph. This will remove much of the uneven areas.

A dry Scotch Brite® abrasive pad is then gently rubbed on the carving to further smooth it.

Rubbing a slightly dampened plastic sponge on the carving completes the final burnishing. Care must be taken not to rub too vigorously as the rubbing can alter the shape of the carving. This step may not be necessary for all carvings.

The starfish is being painted with a blue acrylic paint. The color is obtained by mixing ultramarine blue with titanium white.

The central top starfish is carved from the full sized soap pattern. The blue starfish is carved from the square pattern shown in this book. The red starfish is carved from a third pattern not shown in this book. Other starfish are different shades of brown.

Chapter Three
Sperm Whale

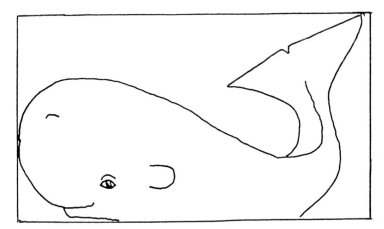

Techniques described

1. *Caricature carving*
2. *Relief carving*
3. *Using a single bar of Ivory Soap® to make the carving*
4. *Using dressmakers' pins as eyes*

The Sperm Whale, along with the Humpback Whale, are probably two of the best known whales, and are examples of two different groups of whales: the toothed and baleen whales respectively. Both species were heavily hunted during the whaling days. They were hunted primarily for their oil derived from their blubber. The Sperm Whales' teeth were engraved (scrimshawed) by whalers and have become valuable art objects. I have observed and photographed the Humpback Whales while working as an underwater photographer for the Hawaii Whale Research Foundation. However, I have not been able to photograph the elusive Sperm Whale in its natural habitat, despite two trips planned specifically to observe and photograph them.

For a number of years I carved some relief caricatures of the Sperm and Right Whales out of beautiful hardwoods for hanging on the walls. They were fun to carve and relatively easy to make. Because my interests were focused on "stylized realism", I have not spent time expanding that style. I have included a simple caricature carving of a Sperm Whale because it is an excellent style for soap carving.

This will be a relief carving of one half of the whale in caricature style using a single bar of soap. The technique of making and using dressmakers' black-headed pins will be shown.

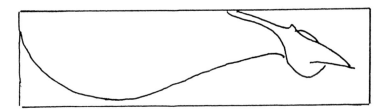

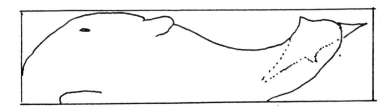

Top, Lateral (side) view; second level, Dorsal (top) view; third level, Ventral (abdominal) view; bottom, Frontal view.

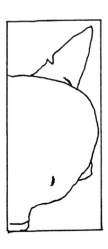

References

Ellis, Richard. *The Book of Whales*. New York, New York: Alfred A. Knoff, pp. 100-121, 1980.

Suzuki, Howard K. *The Carver's Book of Aquatic Animals*. Atglen, Pennsylvania: Schiffer Publishing, Ltd., 1995.

Scrape Ivory Soap® logo off of one side of the soap bar. The side with the logo retained will essentially not be carved, except for the fluke ("tail") and caudal peduncle area (the narrowed junction between the fluke and body).

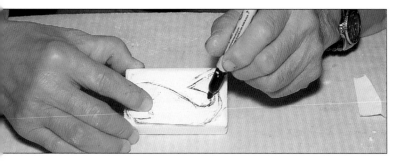

The pattern on the soap is made more visible with a black marking pen after the outline is grooved with a wooden needle so that the outline could be more easily seen in the photograph. However, it is not necessary for you to mark the outline with a pen.

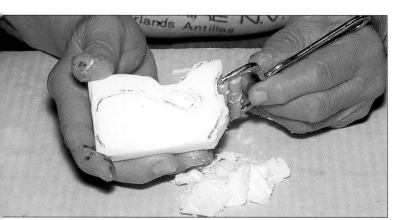

Rough out the whale outline using a cheese cutter or a straight blade knife.

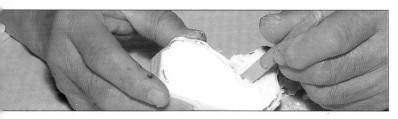

Use a shallow gouge and cheese cutter to carefully widen the space between the body-caudal peduncle junction and the fluke.

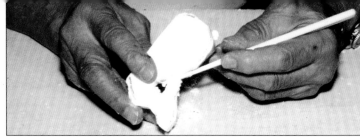

Carefully widen and shape the intervening space between the body and the caudal peduncle and fluke.

Lateral (side) view of the carving at this stage of the carving.

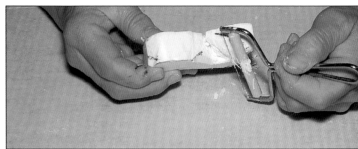

Turn the carving to show top view of the whale. The fluke is to be facing up towards the back at an oblique angle. A cheese-cutting tool is used to carve out the front part of the skewed position of the fluke.

Following the same angle, remove soap from the other side of the fluke.

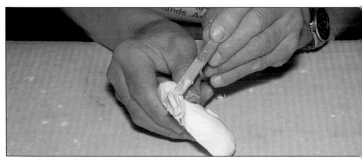

Shape the caudal peduncle (junction of body and fluke) making it narrower to look more like a "stalk" holding the fluke to the body.

Use a shallow gouge to carve sharp peaked central ridges oriented to the midline of both surfaces of the fluke. The dorsal and ventral ridges become less pronounced as they blend going forward into the caudal peduncle and end at the mid-body region.

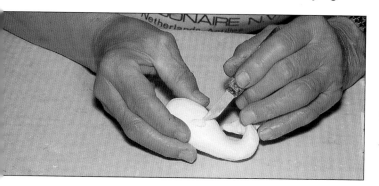

Outline the pectoral fin and carve to make it standout from the body. Remember this is a relief carving so do not detail or carve the pectoral fin on the other side.

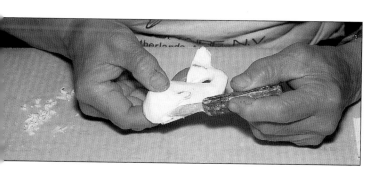

Locate the mouth on the bottom of the carving, and carve a narrow half mouth since this is a relief carving.

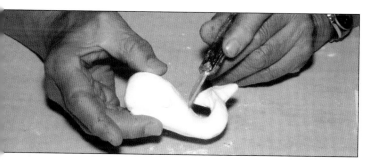

Use a skew blade to do the initial smoothing of the carving. Note that the shapes of the pectoral fin and mouth.

Sandpaper (150-180 grit) and/or an abrasive pad may be used to further smooth the carving.

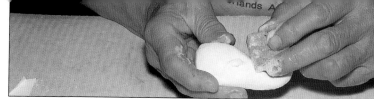

A damp sponge is rubbed over the carving for final burnishing of the carving.

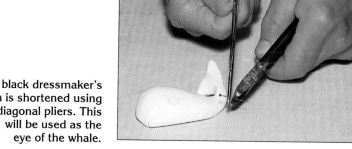

A black dressmaker's pin is shortened using diagonal pliers. This will be used as the eye of the whale.

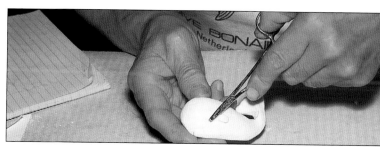

The eye is inserted into the eye area using a hemostat or fine forceps.

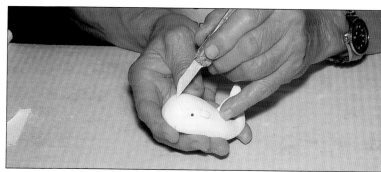

A small curved groove is made near the top of the left side of the head and will represent the off center blowhole located on the left side of the head.

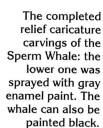

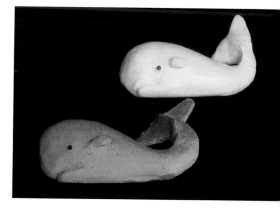

The completed relief caricature carvings of the Sperm Whale: the lower one was sprayed with gray enamel paint. The whale can also be painted black.

Chapter Four
Sea Otter

Special Techniques

1. This is an example of deep-relief carving in which only part of the body is exposed and carved. The sea otter is" floating" in water with only its abdominal surface, head and extremities seen.

2. Pins were punched through the pattern to locate positions of underlying structures on the carving.

3. A hand made mini-wire brush was devised to texture fur on the carving.

4. Adding vibrissae or chin hairs is described.

5. Fur is simulated by scoring a mini-brush on the carving.

6. A base was made by fusing two Ivory Soap® bars side-by-side to make it larger. It was then carved to shape and appropriately painted.

A few years ago while teaching a seminar near Otis, Oregon, I saw my first wild Sea Otter floating offshore. More recently in 2005 I observed several in a bay near Seward, Alaska. They were floating on their backs with their arms resting on their chests and their hind limbs sticking out of the water. This is a very common position that the Sea Otter often takes. The body is well insulated, but the limbs are not as well insulated; therefore, they keep their limbs out of the water as much as possible. Unlike the River Otter, the Sea Otter can live their entire life in the water without coming to shore. In my previous book, *Carving in Soap: North American Animals*, I included the carving of a standing River Otter. Both otters are delightful animals to carve.

The floating Sea Otter is an excellent example of deep relief carving. I am using one commonly observed position. By obtaining the books listed below, you can get other fascinating poses of the Sea Otter, such as one holding an abalone on its chest, or a mother otter with the baby resting on the mother's chest.

After carving the Sea Otter, a texturing tool that was devised to simulate their fur as commercial wire brushes were too coarse and big to use. A mini-wire brush was made from copper strands of an electric cord. Its construction is described in Chapter One.

References

Leon, Vicki, Bucich, R. and Foott, J. *A Raft of Sea Otters: An Affectionate Portrait*. San Luis Obispo, California: Blake Publishing, 1988

Paine, Stephanie and Foott, Jeff. *The World of the Sea Otter*. San Francisco, California: Sierra Club Books, 1993.

Suzuki, Howard K. *Carving in Soap: North American Animals*. Atglen, Pennsylvania: Schiffer Publishing Ltd., 2001.

Resting Sea Otter in the Alaska Kenai Fjord National Park

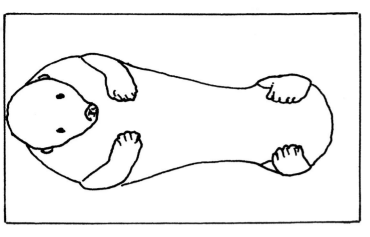

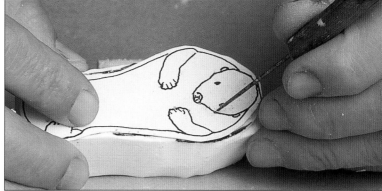

Carve the Sea Otter to the outline of the pattern. Punch needle holes through the pattern over the outlined carving to locate the positions of the head and limbs on the soap-carving pattern.

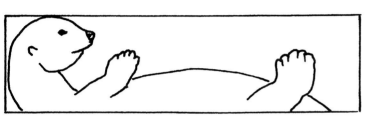

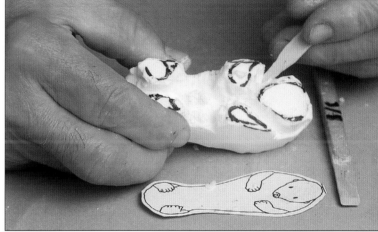

Outline the locations of the head and limbs using the pinholes to outline their relative positions. Then carve around the outlined head and limbs as shown.

Top, Ventral (abdominal) view; middle, Lateral (side) view; bottom, Frontal view

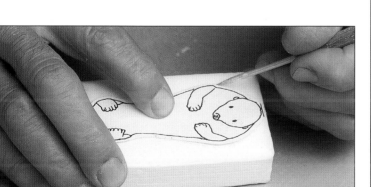

Outline the Otter pattern on the soap, which just had the logo scraped off.

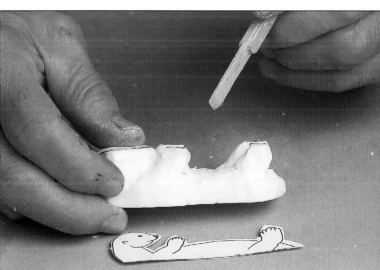

Lateral view showing the roughed out carving of the head and limbs: note that the limbs are not shortened or detailed at this time.

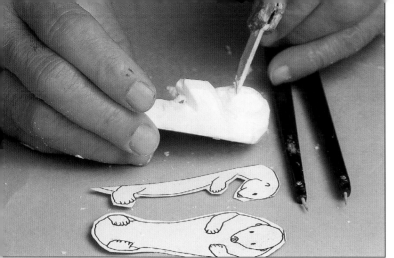

Shape the head, beginning to round it.

The basic appearance of the carving completed at this stage.

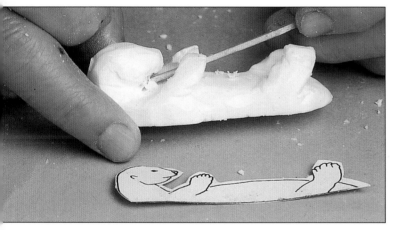

Continue shaping and undercutting the chin and neck areas. Shape the limbs to curve toward the chest. Shorten the limbs by carving them to their proper proportions.

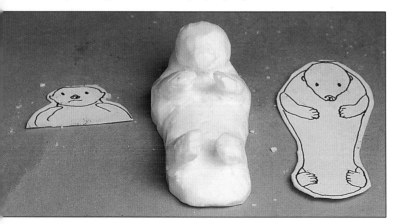

Caudal view of carving showing curved limbs and general shape of the head.

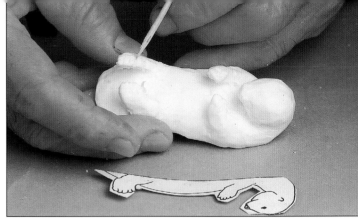

Further shape the limbs and detail the paws by grooving them with a wooden needle.

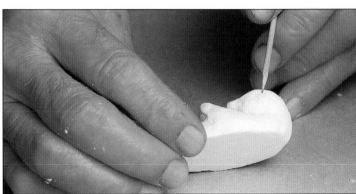

Outline the ears and carefully remove soap from edges of the ears to make them stand out.

Mark location of the eyes.

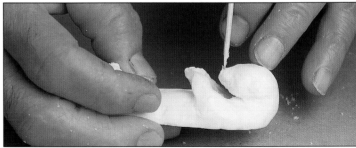

Make shallow grooves to outline the nose and mouth.

Paint location of the eyes black. The painted eyes will be replaced by wired eyes made out of black dressmaker's pins.

Caudal-superior view of completed unpainted Sea Otter

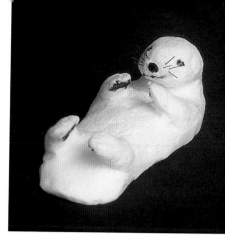

Texture "fur" using a mini-copper braided wire brush by scratching the mini-brush over the surface of the carving.

The base is made by fusing two Ivory Soap® bars side-by-side as shown. *Review the technique of fusing soap bars described in Chapter One on Some Special Techniques.*

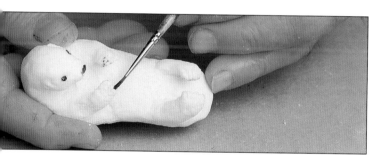

Paint the nose, mouth, and paws with black enamel.

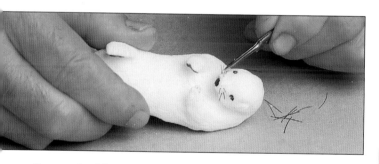

Use a pair of forceps to insert cut hairs from a disposable glue brush on the jaw area. For finer hairs, make shallow holes using a needle made from a silk pin attached to a dowel. Heavier hairs can be pushed into the soap without making a starter hole. *This technique is described more fully in Chapter One in the section Adding Vibrissae.*

After the base is fused, carve it to the desired shape. Paint the base blue using the method described for painting the Blue Starfish in Chapter 2. The Sea Otter is then painted a dark brown mottled color and placed on the blue "ocean" base.

Superolateral view of completed unpainted Sea Otter

Chapter Five

Manatee

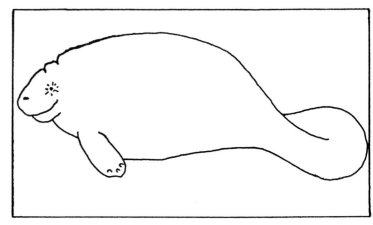

Special techniques

1. In-the-round carving using a single bar of Ivory® soap bar is described

2. Common pinhead is dipped in black enamel to make eyes for the manatee

3. A base is made out of multiple bars of soap and painted to simulate a limestone rocky bottom.

The Manatee is a most interesting marine animal. It belongs to the Family Sirenidae and interestingly is related to the elephants. An elongated round body, round horizontal flexible tail, short forelimbs and a rather blunt shaped head with highly flexible upper jaws, characterizes them. They are found along the coasts of Florida and Central and South America. Many tourists flock to the Crystal River area on the Gulf Coast of Florida to observe and swim with them. A closely related species called the Dugong is found in the Middle East and South Pacific.

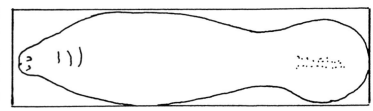

Reference

Suzuki, H.K. *The Carver's Book of Aquatic Animals*. Atglen, Pennsylvania: Schiffer Publishing, Ltd., 1995.

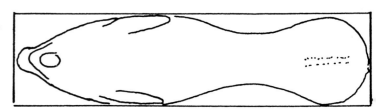

Top, Lateral (side) view; next level, Dorsal (back) view; third level, Ventral (abdominal) view; bottom, Frontal view.

Manatee mother nursing her baby in Crystal River, Florida

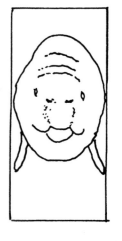

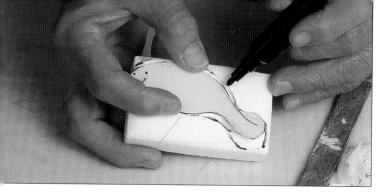

Score the outline of the side view of the manatee pattern with a wooden needle on a previously scraped Ivory Soap® bar. A black marking pen was used only to make it easier for the viewer to see the outlined manatee.

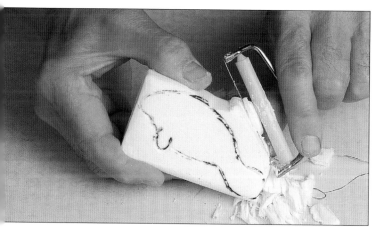

Carve soap to the outlined manatee using a cheese cutter or straight bladed knife.

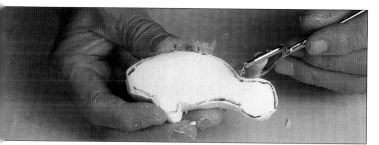

Side view of carved outlined manatee

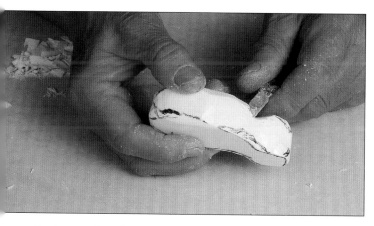

Begin rounding the manatee carving.

Rear view of manatee. Carve the tail at an angle from the body axis and then round the margin of the tail.

Use a deep gouge to remove the soap between the attachments of the pectoral fins to the body.

Outline the lower jaw.

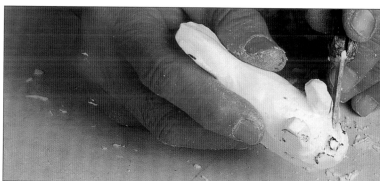

Mark the upper jaw and carve along the curved outline of the upper jaw. Then carve around the outline of the round lower jaw.

Use shallow gouge to carve shallow concavities on each outer side of the upper jaw.

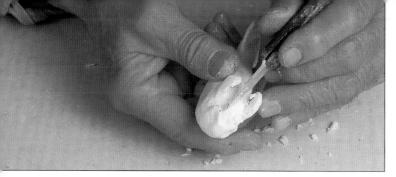

Carve the margin of the lower jaw to give it a convex appearance. Remove material behind the lower jaw prominence.

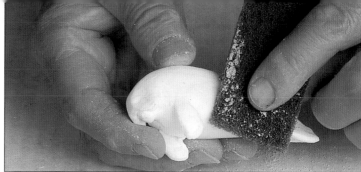

Smooth or start the initial burnishing using an abrasive pad.

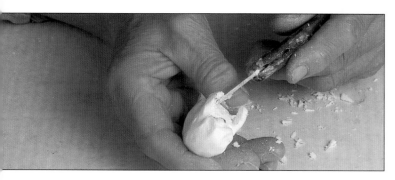

Carve the fins to curve slightly inward so that the inner surfaces will be concave.

Now rub a moist plastic sponge over the carving. Do not rub too vigorously, you will dissolve too much of the carving.

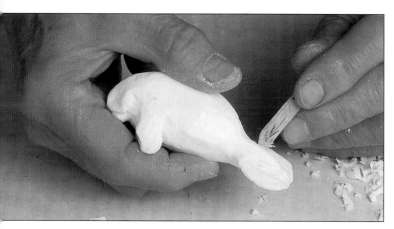

Detail the tail by first carving a central longitudinal ridge and then tapering the tail towards its margin. Note the appearance of the upper and lower jaws in the head region and the shape of the fin.

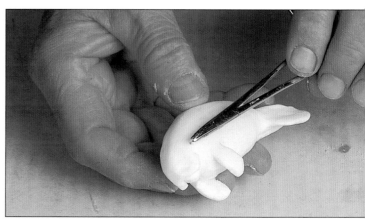

Select pins that had their heads dipped in black enamel and dried. Insert the cut shortened "black eye" pins in the carving head where the eyes should be located.

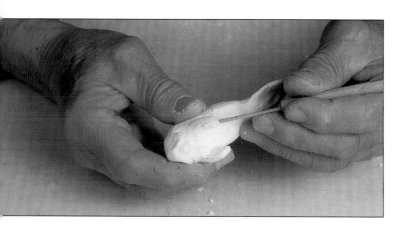

Continue shaping the pectoral fins.

Score a pair of U-shaped grooves, representing nasal openings in the nose area (rostrum).

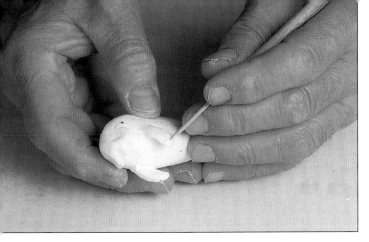

Make four tiny U-shaped grooves on flippers to represent nails.

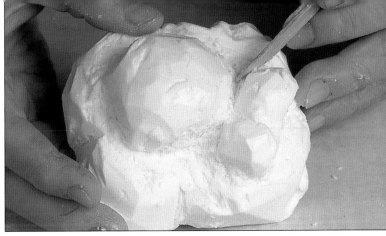

Carve irregularly shaped rock-like limestone base.

Right lateral view of completed unpainted manatee

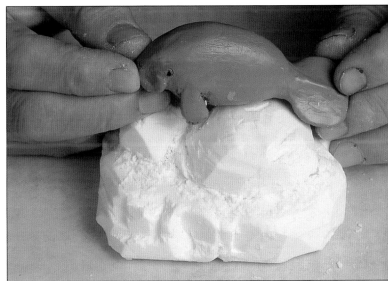

Carve the support part of the base to fit the shape of the abdominal surface of the manatee.

Soften the long narrow edges of two Ivory Soap® bars by placing them vertically on a plate holding some water. Glue the two softened edges together. The two bars may have two wooden pins inserted to strengthen the joint. Fill the joint with soap paste. Cut three irregularly shaped pieces of soap from another bar. Glue them on the "double-wide" soap bar base.

Spray the Manatee with Testors® gray enamel paint (# 1237). Lightly paint the entire base with diluted burnt sienna water-color paint to simulate limestone rocks covered with some algae or plant growth.

Chapter Six
Queen Angelfish

Techniques used

1. In-the-round carving
2. Single bar of soap used
3. Simple unpainted soap bar base made to display the fish

The beautiful Angelfish is probably the first tropical fish that first-time snorkelers or scuba divers see when they get into the shallow waters of tropical corals reefs throughout the world. They are large, slow moving, and are, in general, spectacularly colored. I found that the Indo-Pacific oceans have a much wider mind-boggling variety of angelfish than found in the Caribbean. The Angelfish is also popular in the collections of personal salt water aquaria.

The Angelfish has a laterally compressed, disc-like body, with a small protruding mouth that looks like it is puckering for a kiss (i.e., in an anthropomorphic sense). They vary from one to two feet in size. The young fish have different colorful patterns than that of the adults. The adults are often seen in pairs. The older adults develop long lance-like extensions on their dorsal and ventral fins.

The Queen Angelfish was selected for this book because it represents a well-known tropical fish group that is easily identifiable by its unique shape. A photograph of a young French Angelfish is shown with its slightly different shape of the caudal edge of the dorsal and ventral fins. The carving design will be that of a younger Queen Angelfish so that we will not have to deal with the delicate lance-like extensions of the dorsal and ventral fins.

References

Böhlke, J. and C.C.G. Chaplin. *Fishes of the Bahamas and Adjacent Tropical Waters*. Austin, Texas: University of Texas Press, pp. 412-419, second edition, 1993.

Talbot, Frank and Roger Steene. *Reader's Digest Book of the Great Barrier Reef*. Sydney, Australia: Reader's Digest, 1984.

Immature French Angelfish, Bahamas

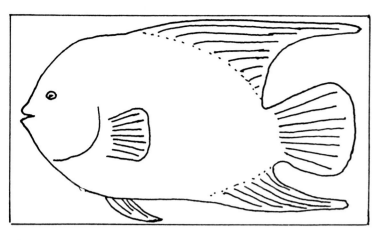

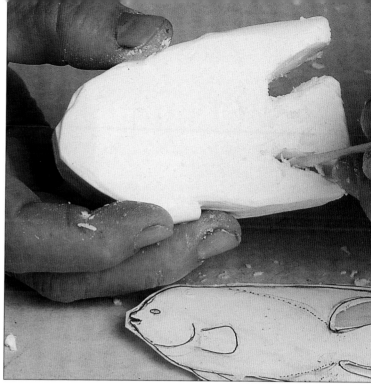

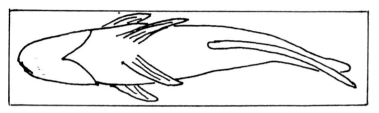

Carve the outline of the angelfish and use wooden needle to remove soap between narrow spaces between the dorsal and ventral fins and the caudal peduncle.

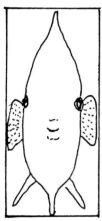

Top, Lateral (side) view; middle, Ventral (abdominal) view; lower, Frontal view.

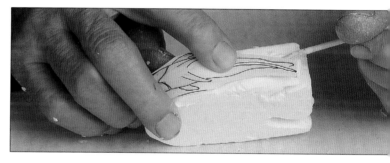

Place ventral surface pattern on abdominal surface of the carving, and outline the pattern on the carving with a wooden needle.

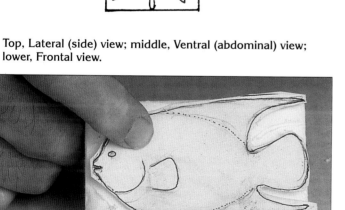

Place lateral view pattern on an Ivory Soap® bar that had its logo scraped off. Outline the pattern on the soap using a wooden needle.

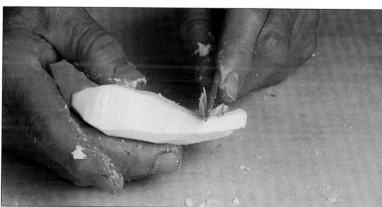

Carefully carve up to the transferred lines from the ventral surface pattern paying particular attention to the tail and fins.

Locate position of left pectoral fin by puncturing pinholes in pattern placed over the carving. The pinholes will locate the margin of the pectoral fin on the carving.

Use the needle to outline the position of the left pectoral fin on the carving.

Turn the body over and use the opposite side of the pattern, and repeat steps 7 and 8. Use the previously made holes to locate the site of the right pectoral fin. Note that the abdominal surface is facing up in this photo.

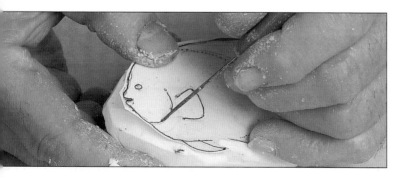

Turn the body over to the left side again and place pinholes in pattern locating the gill cover margins.

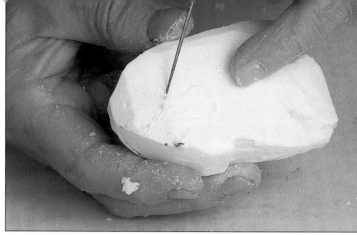

Groove locations of gill plates on both sides.

Undercut the margins of the gill plates, and pectoral fins. Then begin shaping and thinning dorsal and ventral fins.

Turn the body with the abdominal surface up and undercut the margins of the gill plate and extend them to the sides of the body.

Carefully shape and detail the dorsal and ventral fins and tail. Make only thin shavings, as the fins are very friable. Do not attempt to carve the fins too thin, and use only sharp tools. Hone and clean your carving tools frequently. While I do not recommend that young children use sharp steel knives, cleaner and more delicate cuts can be made with them.

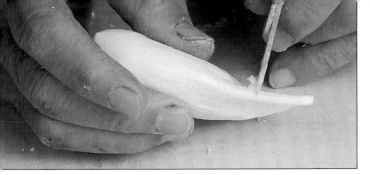

Round the edges of the fins to make them appear thinner.

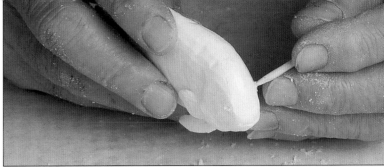

Locate and make depressions to locate eye sockets and insert shortened black dressmakers pins into identified eye sockets.

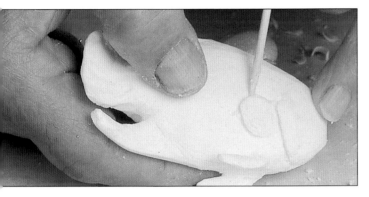

Undercut the edges of the pectoral fins and gill plates to make them stand out more.

This photograph, with a Manatee carving, shows a general-purpose support and base for soap carvings. The Angelfish will be mounted on such a base. The base is made by scraping the logo off of the Ivory Soap® bar and carving it to an elliptical shape. The upper edge of the base is rounded. The support piece is made by cutting off a piece of the soap bar and shaping it to support the subject. Sandpaper and abrasive pad, as seen in the photograph, are used to burnish the base and support by gentle rubbing of the surfaces. The carving is mounted on the support by inserting a shortened pointed round toothpick into both the carving and support piece. The support piece is held on to the base by a similarly inserted shortened, pointed toothpick.

Simulate fin rays by carefully grooving` shallow parallel lines similar to the pattern drawings. Using a metal needle can make more delicate rays, but a wooden needle is probably safer to use.

Painted Queen Angelfish mounted on general purpose base.

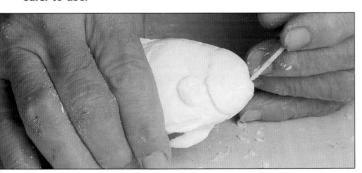

Locate, groove, and shape upper and lower jaws using a wooden needle tool.

Chapter Seven

Clownfish

Techniques Used

1. In-the-round carving
2. Single bar of soap used

I chose the clownfish primarily because it has become well known as "Nemo" in the Walt Disney movie. It is also popular among the salt-water fish aquaria aficionados. The fish is native to the warm waters of the Indo-Western Pacific oceans, including the Red Sea. I have had the privilege of observing and photographing them while scuba diving in the Red Sea, Great Barrier Reef of Australia, and the Fiji Islands. The species vary in color and pattern, but they are always bright and a delight to observe.

The clownfish belongs to the damselfish group, which has worldwide distribution. There are some twenty-seven known species of clownfish classified into a separate sub-family of the damselfishes. What makes the clownfish unique is its symbiotic relationship with the sea anemones; therefore, its other common name is the *Anemone Fish*. The sea anemone protects the clownfish from predators and protects its eggs, while the clownfish helps bring food to the anemone. However, while the anemone can live without the clownfish, the latter cannot live its entire life without the anemone. Like damselfish in general, they are very territorial and will dart back and forth protecting their territory.

This book will describe the carving and painting of one species of clownfish that is found in the Great Barrier Reef of Australia. However, the book will illustrate a couple of other species, so that you have the opportunity to paint the species of clownfish that you would like.

References

Jacques Cousteau The Ocean World. New York, New York: Harry N. Abrams, Inc, pp. 152-158, 1985.

Talbot, Frank and Roger Steene. *The Reader's Digest Book of the Great Barrier Reef*. Sydney, Australia: Reader's Digest, pp. 275-277, 1984.

Clownfish, Fiji Islands, South Pacific

Clownfish protecting its Blue Sea Anemome, Great Barrier Reef, Australia

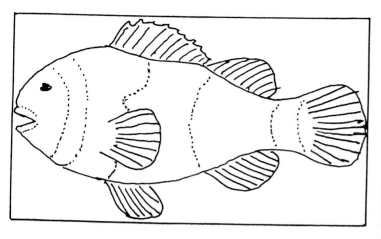

Place pattern on side of Ivory Soap® bar with its logo scraped off. The outline is accentuated with a black marking pen.

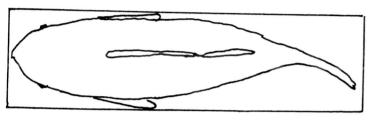

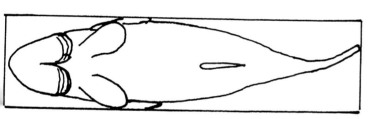

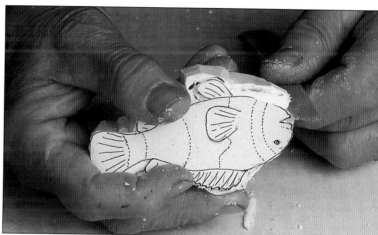

Carve the outline using a straight blade knife.

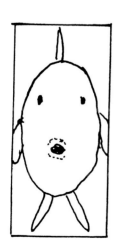

Top, Lateral (side) view; second level, Dorsal (back) view; third level, Ventral (abdominal) view; bottom, Frontal view.

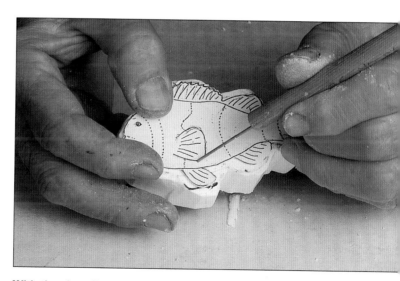

With the clownfish pattern still on the carving, punch shallow holes where pectoral fins are to be located. Turn the pattern over, and repeat on the other side.

Outline the positions of the pectoral fins on both sides using a wooden needle.

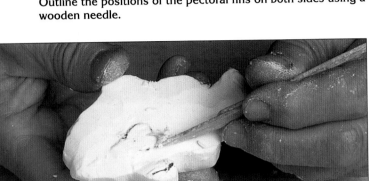

Carve soap from the outer margins of the pectoral fins to make them stand out from the body. Rough out the positions of the pelvic (ventral) fins to look like a V-shape when seen from the front of the fish.

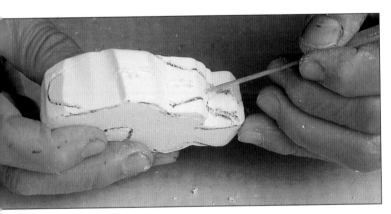

Place dorsal view pattern over the roughed out fish, and mark the outline on the carving. Carve out the sides of the carving to match the top view pattern.

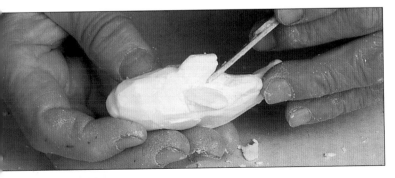

Turn the carving on to its abdominal side and rough out the anal (medial ventral) fin by carving away soap from both sides of the fin. Then carve a V-shaped segment between the paired pelvic fins, located in front of the anal fin.

Start initial rounding of the body by scraping with a skew tool. This view shows the frontal view of general positions of the pelvic fins and dorsal fin.

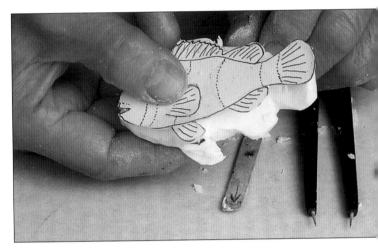

Continue shaping the fish to match the lateral view pattern. Frequently check the progress by overlaying the pattern over the carving.

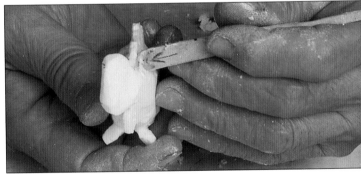

A caudal (tail) view of the carving showing a 0.375" wide round-edged flat tool used to shape the base of the dorsal fin to blend with the curvature of the body. The ventral fin had been previously shaped.

Score fine lines on the dorsal fins to represent the fin rays.

Groove the rays on the tail.

Make similar grooves on the pectoral and pelvic fins.

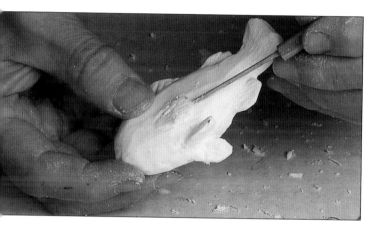

Use a pointed wooden needle to undercut the margins of the pectoral fins using a wooden needle to make them stand out from the body.

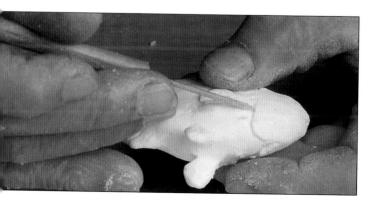

Outline sides and undersurfaces of gill plate margins, and follow them by undercutting those margins.

Carve the borders of the upper and lower jaws. The mouth opening (oral cavity) is formed by digging a small hole between the upper and lower jaws as shown in the photograph.

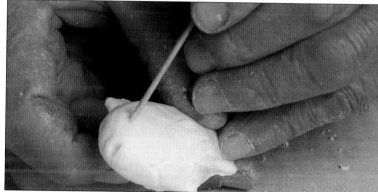

Mark locations of eyes by making small depressions with a needle.

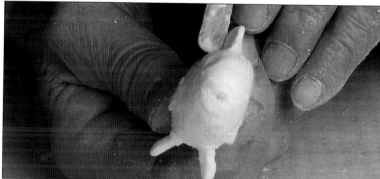

Correct any asymmetries on the body. In this carving it was necessary to reshape the body slightly and re-groove the rays on the repositioned dorsal fin rays.

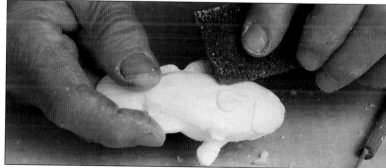

The carving is being smoothed using an abrasive pad. Then the carving is burnished further by rubbing with a damp plastic sponge.

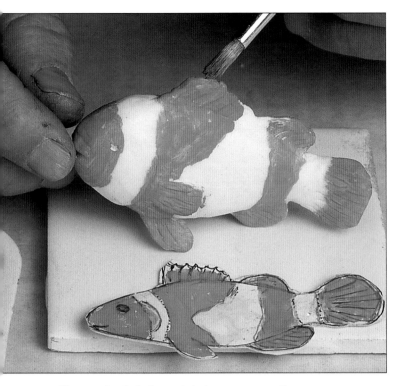

The carving is being painted an orange pattern.

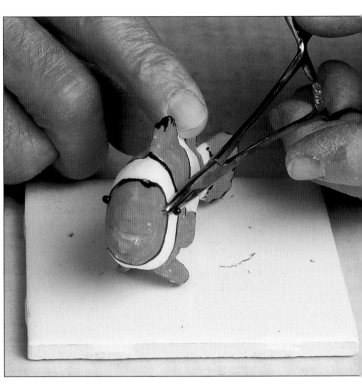

Shortened black dressmakers' pins are inserted to represent the Clownfish eyes.

Black stripes are painted between the white and orange borders.

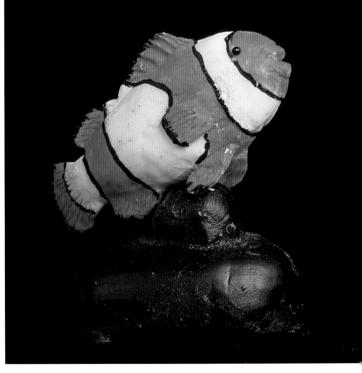

Completed painted Clownfish: the base is made out of two pieces of Ivory Soap® described in the Angelfish chapter and painted with black enamel.

Chapter Eight
Seahorse

The seahorse is a rather strange looking fish that has a head that resembles a horse. As a result, imaginative artists have created paintings of King Neptune riding a Seahorse. I have seen seahorses while scuba diving on the reefs off of Dominica in the Lesser Antilles. Although difficult to find, they have a worldwide distribution, particularly in the tropical waters. They may be seen in the various sea life parks and aquaria in North America.

The seahorse is unique in that it maintains a vertical orientation, while its head is oriented horizontally. The body and tail are segmented with bony rings, and a spindly prehensile-segmented tail replaces the usual fan-shaped tail in other fish. The seahorse has very delicate translucent fins and is a very poor swimmer. They have a prehensile tail that wraps around seaweeds, twigs, etc. to hold them in place. Because they are such weak swimmers, they are found in areas where the current is weak. The female deposits its fertilized eggs in the pouch of the male, so he becomes "pregnant" and nurtures the development of the eggs until they are hatched.

The seahorse was selected to carve because it is well known and has features that make a unique carving. The seahorse in this book was designed with its tail curved in a concentric circle to fit the shape of the Ivory Soap® bar. The segmentations of the body and tail are easily carved. It is not practical to accurately depict the delicate translucent fins so thicker representational fins are carved. Seahorses may he found in different colors from a drab light olive, brown, to bright red or yellow. I chose to paint the carving a bright yellow.

References

Böhlke, J.E., C.C.G. Chaplin. *Fishes of the Bahamas and Adjacent Tropical Waters*. Austin, Texas: University of Texas Press, pp. 177-184, Second Edition, 1993.

Jacques Cousteau: The Ocean World. New York: Harry N. Abrams, Inc., pp. 90-92, 1985.

Lined Seahorse, Turk and Caicos Islands.
Courtesy of Cindy Lott.

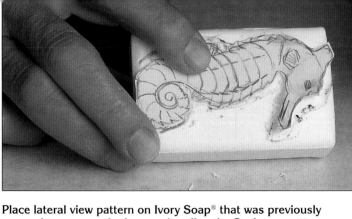

Place lateral view pattern on Ivory Soap® that was previously scraped to remove the logo and outline the Seahorse pattern onto the soap with a wooden needle.

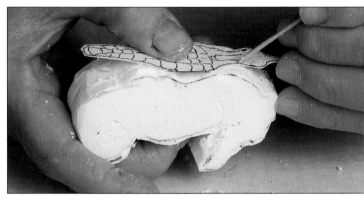

Rough out lateral outline of Seahorse, then place ventral view pattern on back of the carving, and outline the pattern on the carving with a wooden needle.

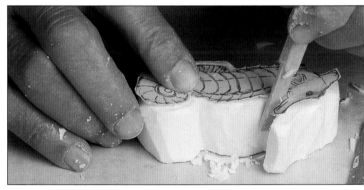

Use a narrow 0.088" wide chisel to carve between the head, neck and the body.

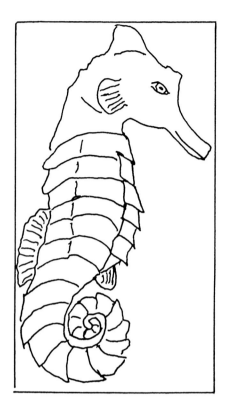
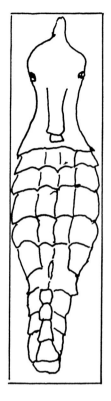
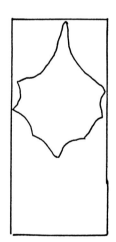

Left top, Lateral view; right top, Ventral view; bottom, Mid-body cross-section.

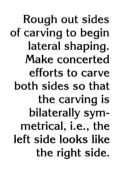
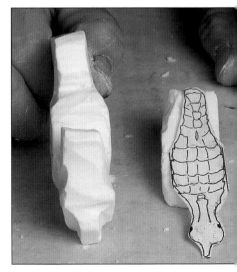

Rough out sides of carving to begin lateral shaping. Make concerted efforts to carve both sides so that the carving is bilaterally symmetrical, i.e., the left side looks like the right side.

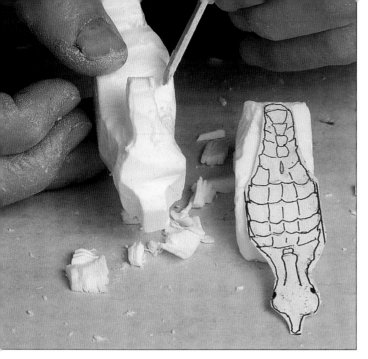

Begin narrowing and shaping the jaws.

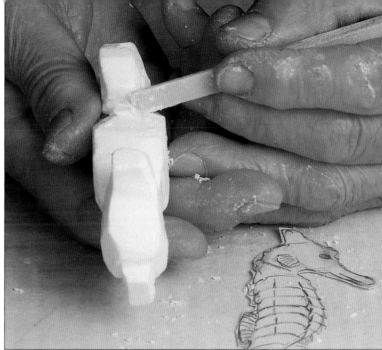

Carve a small median anal fin at the lower end of the abdomen.

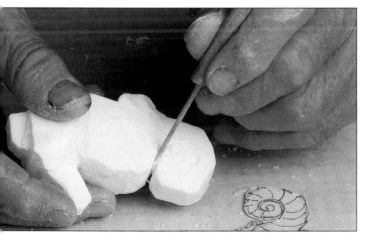

Use a wooden needle to define the body from the curved tail by carving grooves to match the curved configurations of the tail area.

Use a 0.188" wide chisel to detail the tapering as the tail forms a tighter smaller rectangular shaped curl. Use a wooden needle to maintain the outline of the tapering tail.

Use a 0.375" wooden chisel to begin initial tapering of the thickness of the tail as it curls towards the tip of the tail.

Turn the carving so that its dorsal (back) side is up. Shape and thin the median dorsal fin using a 0.375" wooden chisel.

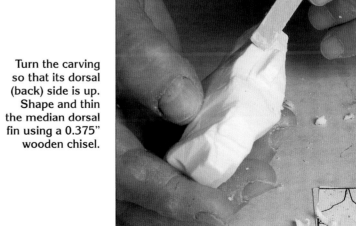

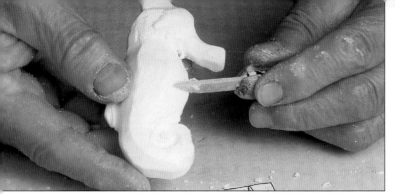

Place the carving on its side, and use a skew shaped blade to carve the body to a general acute angled point at its most ventral part. See cross-sectional drawing.

Round the upper part of the jaw and carve mouth.

Outline pectoral fins and carve around their margins. Next, carve angular cuts similar to the cross-sectional drawing shown and extend caudally towards the base of the tail.

Ventral view of Seahorse with red dressmakers' pins inserted as eyes. Note shape of jaws and mouth.

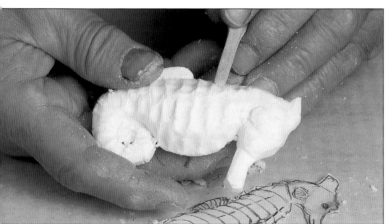

Lateral view of mounted painted Seahorse

With a 0.188" round tip gouge to define the abdomen, sides and back into concave transverse segments. Continue carving the shallow concave grooves into the tail.

Undercut and shape the pectoral fins.

Oblique view of mounted painted Seahorse

Chapter Nine
Emperor Penguin

Techniques

1. In-the-round carving
2. Free standing carving
3. Two Ivory Soap® bars are fused to make a double thickness carving piece
4. Pins are punched through the pattern to locate positions of structures on carving
5. Glass beads are inserted into pins and used as eyes

Penguins have fascinated me for many years and since I have not included them in my prior books, the penguin was one of the first animals selected for inclusion in this book. Some of my early carvings were stylized simple standing penguins similar to the classic Steuben® crystal penguin. Penguins are very popular animals seen in many aquaria and wildlife parks throughout North America.

Penguins are considered to be primitive, flightless sea birds that live in colonies while on land. While clumsy on land, they are very agile swimmers. They need to be fast in the water in order to flee their predators such as sharks, orca, and leopard seals.

Penguins are found only in the southern hemisphere. Here they are widely distributed, but are best known in the Antarctic regions. Their most northern distribution is in the Galapagos Islands off of South America. They are classified in six genera and about eighteen different species. Of that number only four species are known to breed in the Antarctic. I was able to observe and photograph the Galapagos Penguins during an unsuccessful search for the elusive Sperm Whale in the Galapagos Islands.

For this book, a standing Emperor Penguin will be carved. It is the largest of the penguins, and it is found only in the Antarctic. The female lays only one egg, and they breed in the middle of winter, unlike other penguins that lay two eggs and breed in less harsh weather conditions. You may chose to carve a smaller baby penguin and make a mother and baby set. Since I have not ever seen an Emperor Penguin, I am substituting photographs of two Galapagos Penguins as representatives of the Penguin family.

References

The Audubon Society Book of Marine Life. New York, New York: Harry N. Abrams, Inc., pp. 211-213, 1980.
Jacques Cousteau: The Ocean World. New York, New York: Harry N. Abrams, Inc., pp. 351-355, 1985.

Standing Penguin, Galapagos Islands, Ecuador

Diving Penguin, Galapagos Islands, Ecuador

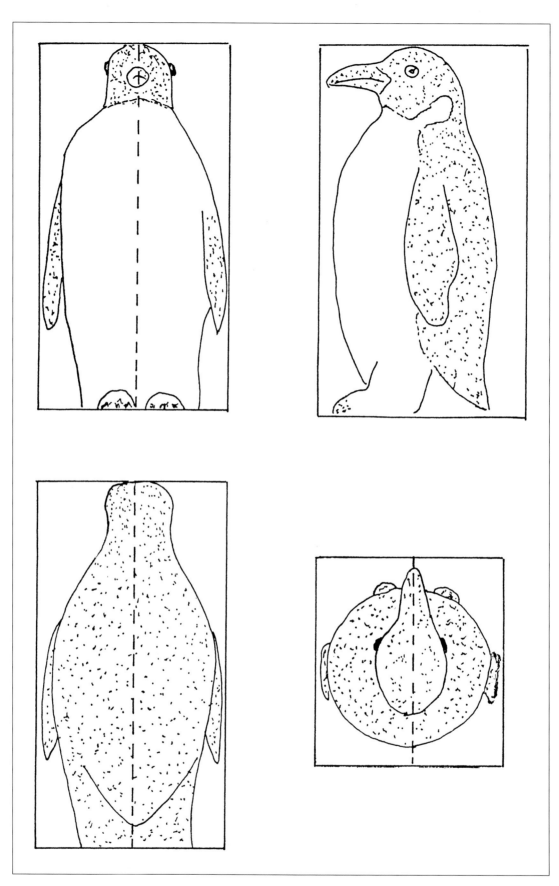

Upper left, Ventral view; upper right, Lateral view; lower left, Dorsal view; lower right, Cranial (head) view.

Scrape two Ivory Soap® bars, removing the logos on both sides of each bar. Place the bars on a dish with a thin layer of water to moisten and soften one side of each bar, before gluing the two bars together.

Place some soap paste on the moistened surfaces of the bars, and press them tightly together. Add soap paste to fill out any spaces between the bars. Place glued bars in a sealable plastic bag, and put aside to allow the bars to meld together. This may take a day or two.

Place lateral view Penguin pattern on the double thickness bar and outline it with a wooden needle.

Trim away the soap around the pattern with right angle cuts. You may wish to use a straight knife on a cutting board.

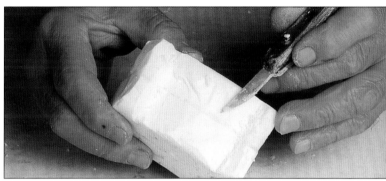

The skew blade is pointing to a minor space between the fused bars. Fill in defects with fresh soap carving scraps by pressing them into the spaces.

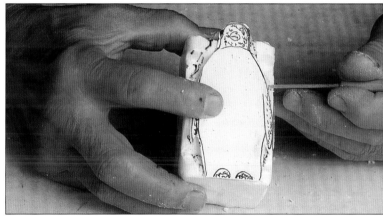

Outline the ventral view pattern on to the carving and shape.

Periodically measure the dimensions of the carving by placing a pair of calipers around various parts of the body and comparing the measurements to the pattern. This procedure helps determine where the penguin has to be shaped further.

Place the lateral view pattern on the carving and locate positions of the wings by punching shallow holes through the pattern where wings are to be located.

Carve the feet.

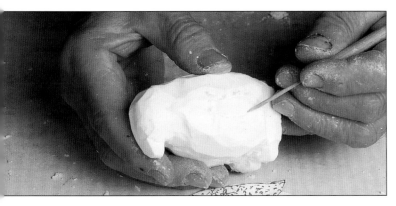

Outline wing locations using the punched holes as guides.

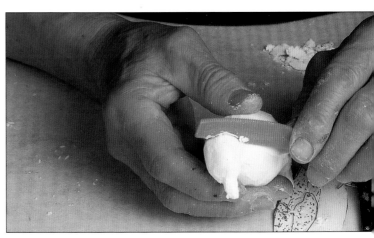

Shape the head and body rounding them with a concave shaped scraper.

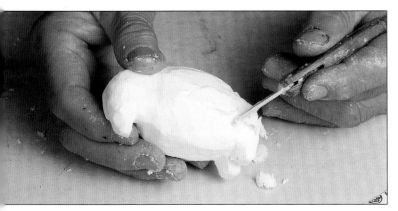

Carve around wing outlines to define them from the body.

Continue shaping and rounding the carving and as it approaches the pattern size, undercut the wings to make them stand out. Continue to shape to reach the proper proportions.

Turn to the dorsal side of the carving and carve the tail.

Ventral view of the roughed out penguin

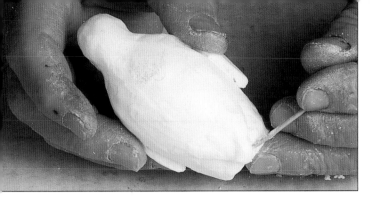

Dorsal view of roughed out penguin showing undercut tail

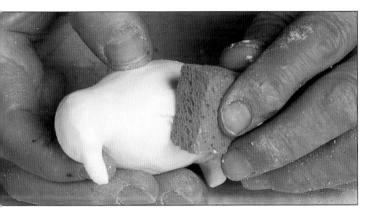

The carving is first smoothed by rubbing an abrasive pad over it. This photo shows the carving being further smoothed using a damp sponge.

Oblique view of Penguin painted with Testors® black enamel
The nape area is brushed with yellow watercolor paint. The white portion of the body is not painted.

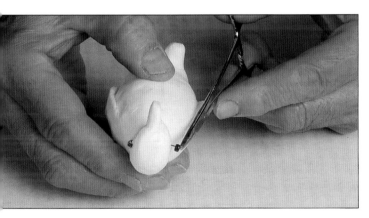

Two black glass beads inserted into shortened silk pins are pushed into the carving to serve as eyes. Black beads are used because the black dressmaker's pinheads are not large enough for this Penguin carving.

Lateral view of completed unpainted Penguin showing shape of wings.

Lateral view of painted Penguin

Chapter Ten
Orca

Special Techniques

1. In-the-round double thickness soap bars carving.

2. Carving mounted on a double bar soap base using soap paste to simulate splashing waves.

The Orca or Killer Whale is well known because it is one of the star attractions in many marine wildlife parks in the United States. They are not whales but actually belong to the dolphin group. In the wild, they have a worldwide distribution adjacent to the various continental shelves of the different continents. They usually travel in groups called pods. Their striking black and white color pattern makes them easy to identify.

A soap carving of an unpainted breaching Orca was included in my previous soap carving book, *Carving in Soap: North American Animals*. The Orca and base were carved as a single carving out of a double-thick soap bar. It included the splashing waves carved out of the same double-fused soap bar.

In this book, the carving will be made from two separate soap bars: the Orca and a base. The carved Orca will be inserted into the carved base and molding soap paste around the attached carving will create the wave splashes. In addition, the Orca and base will be painted to show off its striking contrasting black and white colors. The carving is a female Orca as the adult male's dorsal fin is too long and delicate to carve in soap.

References

Katoma, Steven K., V. Rough, and D.T. Richardson. *A Field Guide to the Whales, Porpoises and Seals of the Gulf of Maine and Eastern Canada, Cape Cod to Newfoundland*. New York, New York: Charles Scribner's Son, pp. 109-117, Second Edition, 1983.

Suzuki, H.K. *Carving in Soap: North American Animals*. Atglen, Pennsylvania: Schiffer Publishing, Ltd., 2001.

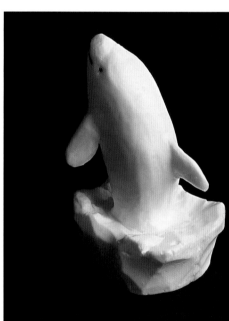

Breaching Orca and base carved as a single unit from double thickness Ivory Soap® bars glued together. This carving was described and illustrated in my previous book, *Carving in Soap: North American Animals*.

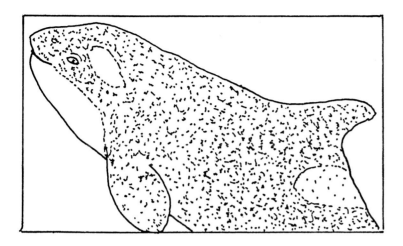
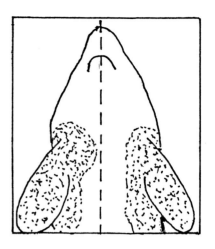
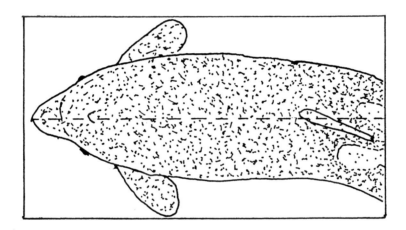

Upper left, left lateral view; upper right, frontal-ventral view; middle, dorsal view; bottom, ventral view.

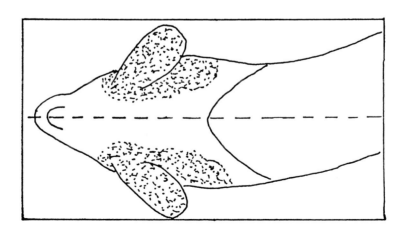

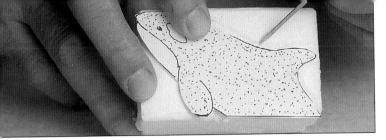

Lateral view of Orca pattern with outline being marked on double thickness soap bars. Making the double thickness bar has been described previously in Chapter 9 on the carving of the Penguin.

Rough out side view using a long straight blade. A cutting board, such as a ceramic tile, may be used to serve as a base to "hog-out" larger segments of soap. "Hogging-out" is a term that is often used to describe removing large chunks of material in the initial stages of roughing out the carving. Care must be taken not to cut through too large a segment of soap, as it might shatter the carving.

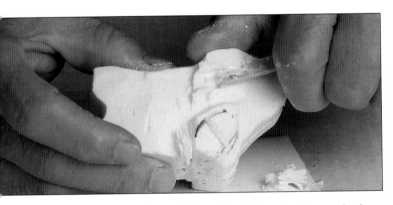

Outline the positions of the pectoral fins using the method previously described for the Sea Otter and the Penguin, by placing the pattern over the carving and punching pinholes where the pectoral fins are located. Rough out the general shape of the pectoral fins.

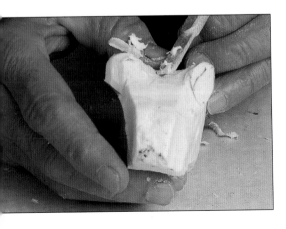

Turn the carving over with its abdominal surface facing up and remove soap between the ventral surfaces of the pectoral fins and chest region.

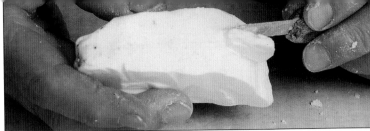

Outline position of medial dorsal fin and remove material from either side of the medial dorsal fin.

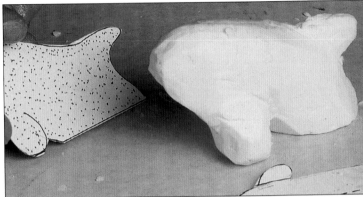

The carving after rounding the back and head.

A wooden needle is shown removing soap from the caudal junction of the pectoral fin from the ventral surface of the body. The pectoral fins are also shaped.

Shape and round the snout.

Carve the mouth and locate the positions of the eyes.

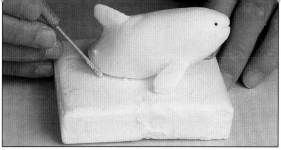

After gluing a doublewide pair of Ivory Soap® bars and allowing the bars to dry, place the Orca carving on the base. Outline the Orca carving on the base of the doublewide glued soap bars. Carve a depression matching the outline of the Orca base. The Orca carving is then inserted into the depression.

Shape and detail the pectoral and dorsal fins by rounding the front of the fins and tapering the caudal margins.

Insert two wooden pins made from shortened pointed tooth picks into the bottom of the carving and tentatively fit the carving into the oval depression in the base.

Use an abrasive pad to smooth the carving and follow it by burnishing it further with a damp plastic sponge.

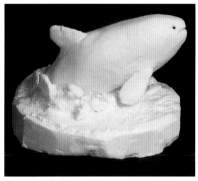

After the carving is fitted well into the base, add slurry of soap paste into the depression, and mount the carving. Add fragments of soap pieces to the slurry to create the waves splashing around the Orca to simulate breaching. Put aside and let the paste harden and dry.

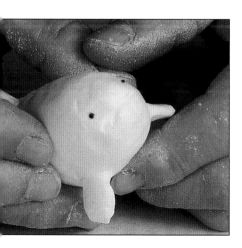

Locate positions of eyes and insert black eyes made from shortened silk pins dipped in black enamel and dried.

The completed painted Orca on a painted base. The carving and base are brush painted with watercolor paints. The white portions are not painted; however, it is recommended that the white part be painted to preserve the soap from discoloration of the exposed unpainted soap surfaces.

Chapter Eleven
Sea Lion

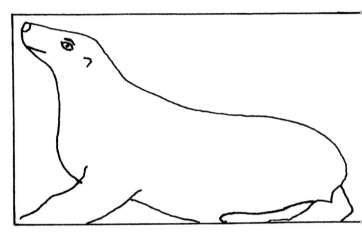

Techniques used

In-the-round carving using a double thick Ivory Soap® bar

Sea lions are popular attractions at various sea aquaria and circuses. They are intelligent, playful and trainable. The sea lions belong to a group of aquatic mammals called the pinnipeds (from Latin feather feet) because they have feather-shaped flippers. The group also includes the various species of fur seals, and the walrus.

I chose the sea lion not only because they are well known and an excellent subject for soap carving, but because I have observed the subspecies of the California Sea Lion on the Galapagos Islands and the Northern Sea Lion in the Gulf of Alaska. In my prior soap-carving book, I described carving the newborn Harp seal.

References

King, Judith E. *Seals of the World.* Ithaca, New York: Comstock Publishing Associates, Second Edition, 1983.
Suzuki, H.K. *Carving in Soap: North American Animals.* Atglen, Pennsylvania: Schiffer Publishing, Ltd., 2001.

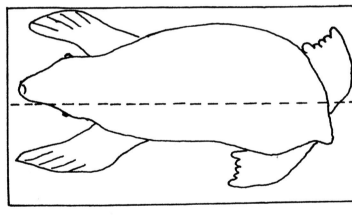

Sea lion, Galapagos Island

Top, Lateral view; middle, Dorsal view; bottom, Frontal view.

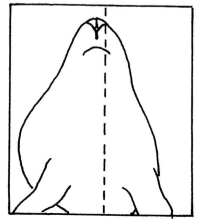

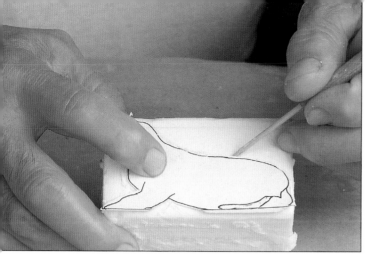

Place the lateral view pattern of the Sea Lion onto a previously made double thickness Ivory Soap® bar. Outline the pattern on to the soap with a wooden needle and carve to the marked lines.

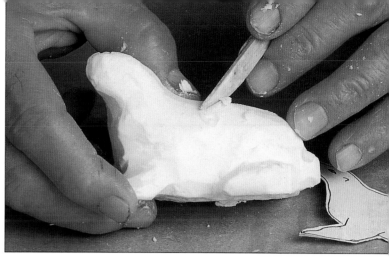

Use a tool, such as a skew, to scrape curves and shape the head, body and flippers.

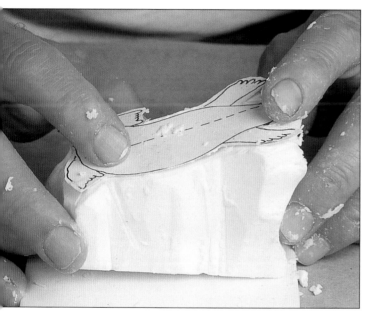

After outlining the dorsal view pattern on the soap, carve to the outline as shown in the photograph.

Carve the tail.

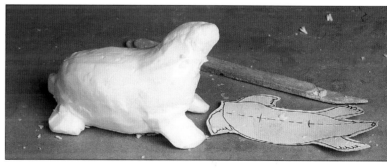

Detail the general configurations of the upper surfaces of the flippers.

Rough out the general shape of the body and head. Locate the general positions of the hind and fore flippers, and carve.

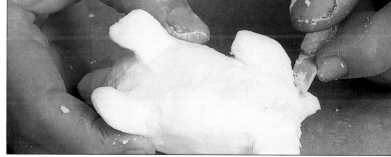

Turn the carving over to its abdominal surface and shape the undersurfaces of the flippers by angling the flippers down and out from the body to the terminal parts of the flippers. Shape the abdomen and neck so that they are rounded. Make smooth transitions from the rounded body to where the flippers join the body. Carve the tail round tapering it to a blunt tip.

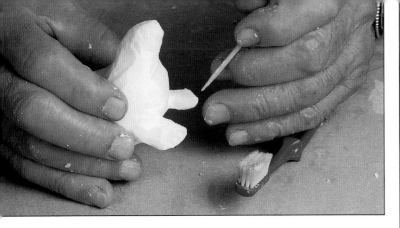

Round the edges of the front flippers and shape as necessary. Make four shallow grooves on the terminal parts of the flippers. These grooves represent the spaces between the underlying digits.

Using a pair of forceps, insert cut hairs from a disposable glue brush into the chin area. *The technique was described in Chapter 1 in the section Adding Vibrissae.*

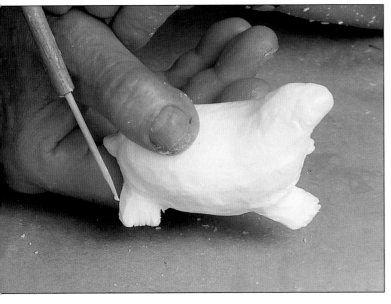

On the hind flippers, keep the inner and outer toes longer than those in-between. Using a needle, make grooves to represent space between the digits.

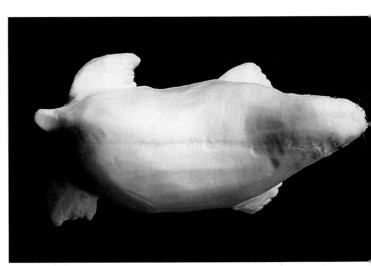

Dorsal view of completed unpainted Sea Lion.

Mark positions of eyes and insert shortened black dressmaker's pins. Groove the nose and mouth and paint them black. Burnish the carving using an abrasive pad. Follow this by rubbing a damp plastic sponge over the carving.

Lateral view of painted Sea Lion.

Chapter Twelve
Beluga

Special Techniques

1. A longer in-the-round carving is described. Two sets of one and a half Ivory Soap® bars are staggered and glued together to lengthen and double the thickness of the carving medium.

2. A piece of 0.75" thick Styrofoam® blue board is made into a base for the Beluga.

The Beluga or White Whale is a medium sized cetacean that is found in the arctic and sub-arctic waters off of Alaska, Russia and eastern Canada. They seasonally migrate north and south in groups according to the ambient temperatures and food sources. The Beluga's most striking feature is that in the adult phase it is completely white. In addition, unlike many of the other whales and dolphins, it does not have a dorsal fin. The young are light brown in color and by their second year turn a bluish gray. They attain their white adult coloration by the seventh year.

The Beluga may be seen in a number of aquaria and sea life parks in the United States and Canada. I have only seen captive Belugas in parks, and never had the pleasure of observing Belugas in the wild.

The Beluga is an ideal subject to carve out of white Ivory Soap® bars since the adult is white in real life. This in-the-round carving utilizes fused, staggered soap bars. The Beluga is then mounted on a Styrofoam® carved base.

References

Ellis, Richard. *The Book of Whales*. New York, New York: Alfred A. Knopf, pp. 91-95, 1980.

Martin, Tony. *Beluga Whale*. World Life Library. Stilllwater, Minnesota: Voyageur Press, 1996.

Martin, Tony. *The World of Whales, Dolphins and Porpoises*. Stillwater, Minnesota, Voyager Press, pp. 60-63, 2005.

Wilkie, S.W. *Whales of the World*. New York, New York: E.J Brill, pp. 208-210, 1988.

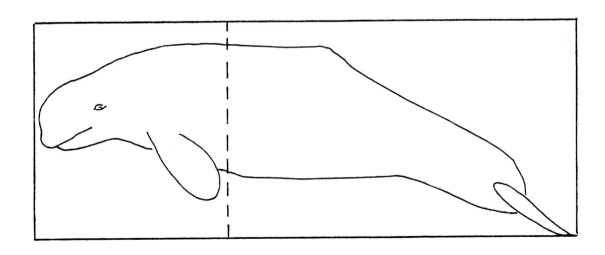

Lateral view

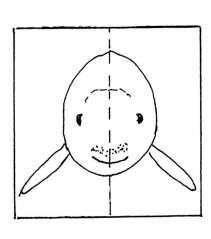
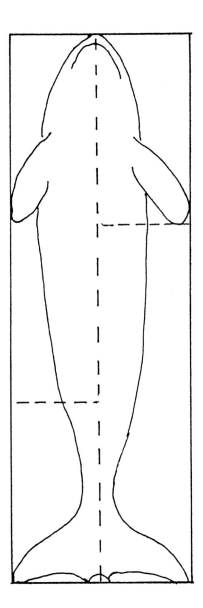
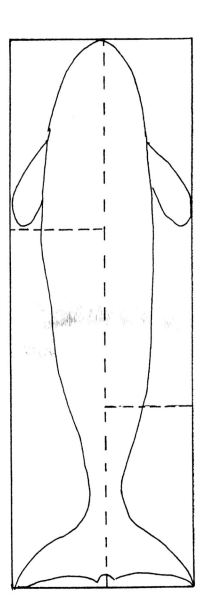

Left, Frontal view; middle, Ventral view; right, Dorsal view.

Scrape the logos off of three Ivory Soap® bars. Cut one bar in half. Square the cut surfaces of the half bars, and one end of the whole bars.

Place the soap bars vertically on a plate that has a shallow layer of water to soften the ends. After the ends are softened, the long and short bars are pressed together to make two elongated soap bars. Then moisten and soften one broad surface on each of the elongated bars in preparation for them to be glued together.

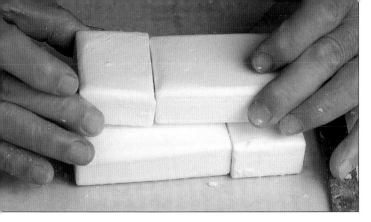

The softened surfaces of the elongated bars are then stacked one on top of the other so that the joints are staggered as shown in the photograph.

After squeezing them together, fill the joint spaces with soap paste as shown in the photograph. Set aside for a day or two in a re-sealable plastic bag to allow the multiple soap bars to fuse and harden.

After outlining the side pattern of the Beluga on the double thickness side of the fused bars, carve to the outlined side view using a long straight bladed sharp knife.

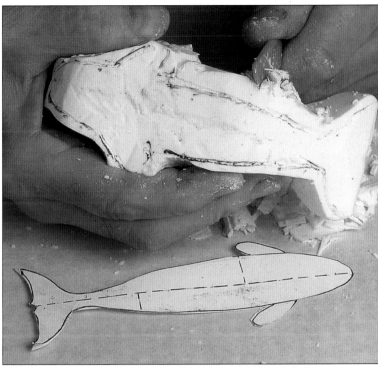

After placing the dorsal view pattern on the carving, carve the outline as shown on the photograph, using the joined surface seam as the centerline.

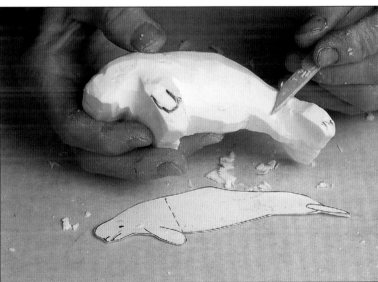

Round the body, and shape the caudal peduncle, fluke and pectoral fins.

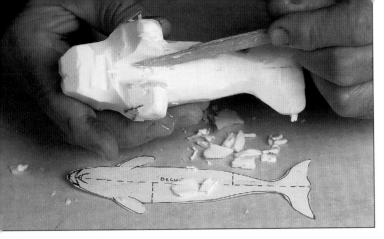

Turn the carving so that the abdominal surface is facing up, and remove material between the pectoral fins. Start rounding the body.

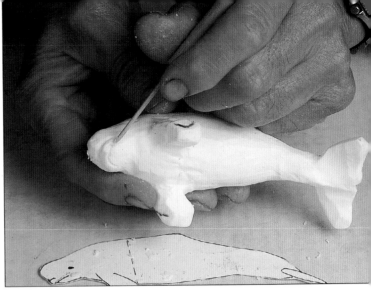

Carve the front of the head to give it a "bulbous" appearance. Then carve a shallow groove at the lower end of the bulge. This will designate the upper margin of the upper jaw. The "bulbous" front of the head and protruding under slung upper jaw are two important identifying characteristics of the Beluga. Groove the mouth using a needle to define it from the lower jaw.

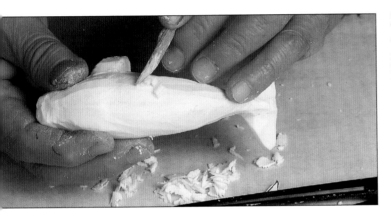

Continue rounding and shaping the entire body and head to match the pattern by using a skew blade in light scraping motions.

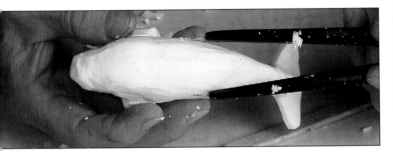

Place the calipers on different parts of the carving as you work and compare those measurements with the patterns. The comparisons help determine where the carving needs to be reconfigured.

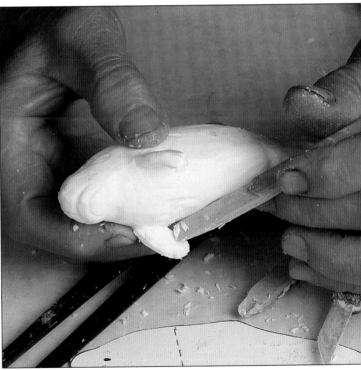

Use a sharp shallow gouge to shape, size and detail the pectoral fins. Give the fins a slight concave curve to make it more lifelike. Be sure to use the calipers to make sure that the two pectoral fins have similar dimensions. Since the soap is very fragile, keep the fins thicker than that found in real life.

Use a shallow gouge to form dorsal and ventral median ridges on the caudal peduncle. Extend the median ridges on to both surfaces of the fluke.

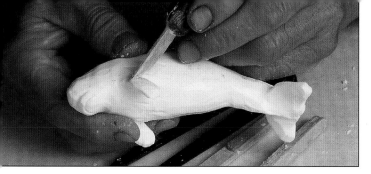

Round the front edges of the fins and taper the back edges. The shape can be comparable to the cross-sectional shape of an airplane wing.

Detail the shape of both surfaces of the fluke. Round the front edge, and taper the back edge. Be sure to retain the central ridges on the base of both surfaces of the fluke. The ridges should end about half the distance from the caudal end of the fluke.

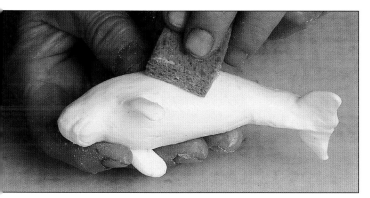

Smooth the carving by first scraping the carving, then using an abrasive pad, and finally rubbing with a damp plastic sponge as shown in this photo.

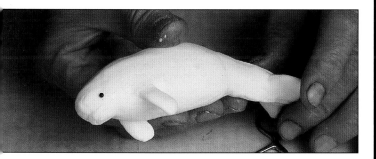

The completed Beluga shown with eyes made out of black dressmakers' pins.

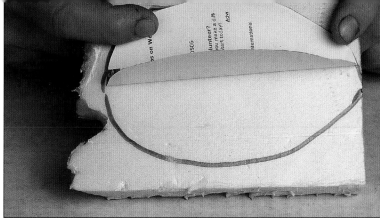

An elliptical pattern is formed by folding a piece of paper and cutting a hemi-elliptical shape. The pattern is unfolded and transferred on to a 0.75" thick piece of blue Styrofoam®. This will form the base of this carving.

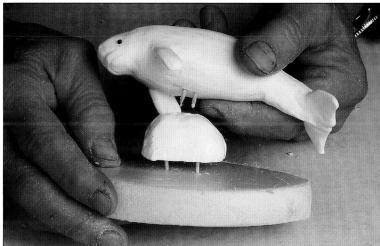

A small piece of Ivory Soap® is carved to hold the carving on the base. Shortened pointed round toothpicks are inserted into the abdominal surface of the Beluga carving. Soap paste is added to the upper surface of the support piece and the carving is pressed on to the support piece. Next, a pair of pointed toothpicks is inserted into the bottom of the support and into the base. The support piece is then pressed on to the base.

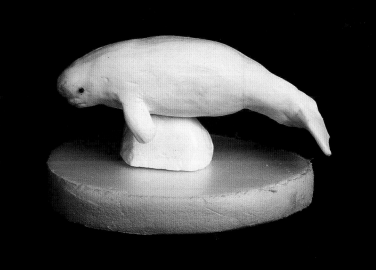

The completed mounted Beluga

Chapter Thirteen
Octopus

Techniques Used

Four and a half Ivory Soap® bars are fused together for a single piece caring.

The octopus is a cephalopod (from the Greek head feet), and is one of the four classes of invertebrates that belong to the Mollusc group. The others include the snails (gastropods), scallops (bivalves), and chitons. They are soft-bodied animals that may or may not have shells.

The octopus has eight legs or tentacles, which are attached to an expansion called the mantle, a modified body. It encloses the urogenital, gastrointestinal and circulatory systems. A separate chamber in the mantle contains the gills. Water passes through openings in the mantle cavity to bring oxygen to the gills and is ejected through the siphon. The ejection of water through the siphon is also used as a means of jet propulsion. The mantle blends in its forward part to become the head, which contains the eyes, brain and mouth. The under-surfaces of the tentacles are full of suckers that help capture prey and bring food to its horny beak. The octopus has special cells in its skin to permit it to change colors very rapidly.

There are about 150 species of octopi in the world. Probably the most well known one is the Giant Pacific Octopus found along the West coast of North America. They are most interesting to observe in their natural habitat. My underwater observations of octopi have been limited to the tropical species inhabiting coral reefs. As a child growing up in Southeastern Alaska, I still remember my father catching the Giant Pacific Octopus hiding in rocky crevices on the seashore during low tide. Octopi are considered delicacies by Asian and Mediterranean people.

The entire Mollusc group would have been fun to carve, but due to space limitations I selected the octopus. My dilemma was to come up with a design that was artistic, doable and not readily breakable. Thus, a swimming octopus with flailing tentacles would not be practical to carve in soap. My solution was to have the octopus resting on a rock. As the last carving presented in this book, I believe it is the most unique and challenging carving. Enjoy!

References

Cerullo, Mary M. and J.L. Rotman. *The Octopus Phantom of the Sea.* New York, New York: Cobblehill Books, 1997.

Talbot, Frank and Roger Steene. *Reader's Digest Book of the Great Barrier Reef.* Sydney, Australia: Reader's Digest Services Pty Ltd., pp. 172-194, 1984.

Zeiller, Walter. *Tropical Marine Invertebrates of Southern Florida and the Bahamas Island.* New York, New York: John Wiley and Sons, 1974.

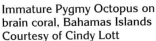

Immature Pygmy Octopus on brain coral, Bahamas Islands
Courtesy of Cindy Lott

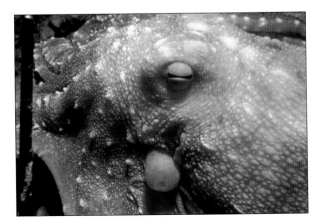

Adult Octopus showing mantle and head
Bonaire, Netherlands Antilles

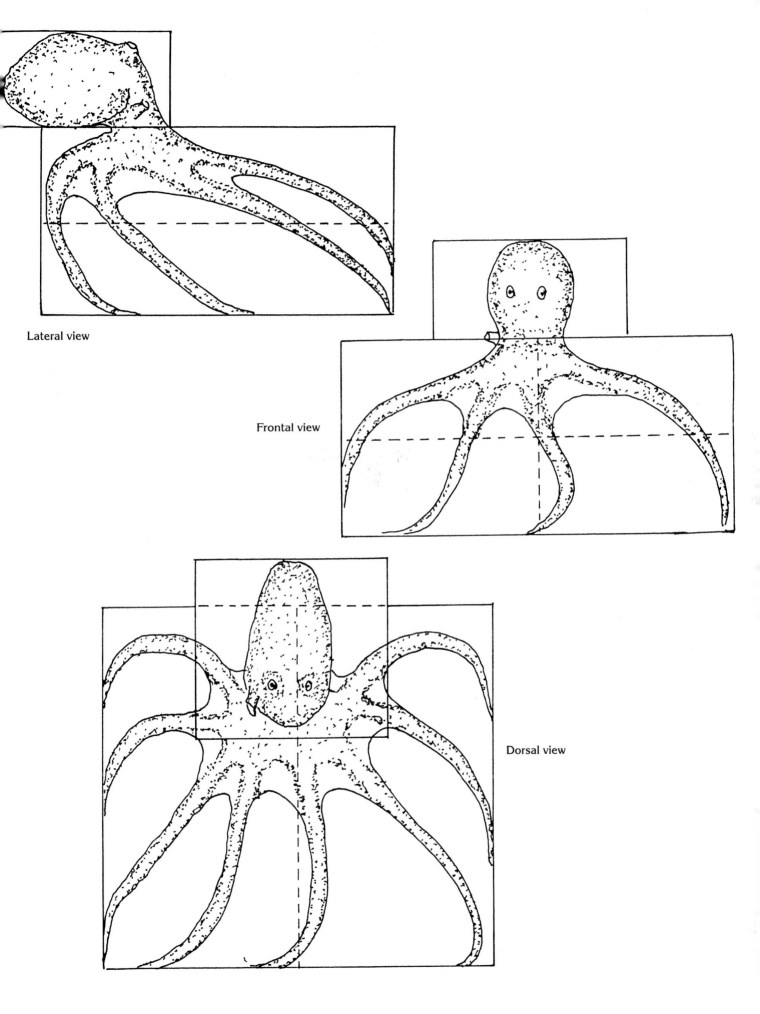

Lateral view

Frontal view

Dorsal view

59

The octopus is made out of four and a half Ivory Soap® bars fused together. Four full bars are prepared as previously described. Each pair is made into a doublewide soap bar pair. Short pointed toothpicks are inserted into the bottom pair, soap paste is placed on the surface, and the second pair of soap bars is placed directly on top of the first pair with the joints aligned.

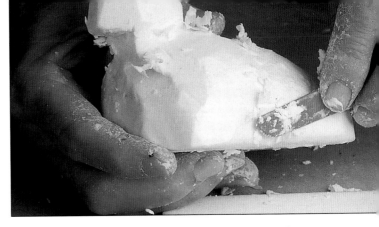

Fill defects on joints with freshly carved soap waste by pressing the soap pieces into the defects.

Attach the prepared half Ivory® bar on the center of the end of the doublewide, double thickness soap bars with 0.75" of the bar extending beyond the end of the multiple bars. Fill the joint gaps with paste soap. Set aside in a sealable plastic bag for one or two days to let the soap bars meld together.

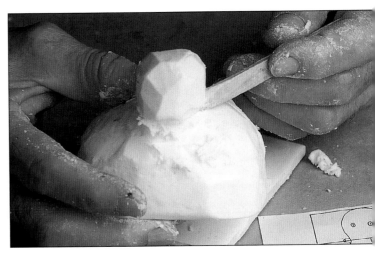

Use a round shallow round tipped flat gouge to carve a narrowed "neck".

After the fused bars have been allowed to harden and fuse, outline the head on the half bar. Then make vertical cuts on the corners of the double thickness soap bars, in order to begin rounding the corners.

Undercut the back of the mantle to round it.

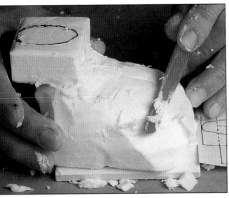

Locate the future placements of the tentacles by carving a downward slope in front of and around the origin of the mantle. Then round the corners of the base of the carving.

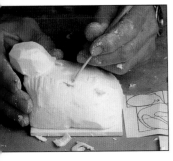

An exposed horizontal pointed toothpick that initially held the upper bars together is shown in the photograph. Since its presence is not essential for the integrity of the carving, it was removed. The defect was filled with soap paste. Continue sloping and curving the front and back of the carving below the head. Follow this by the initial round shaping of the head and mantle.

Outline the margins of the eight tentacles using a wooden needle. The margins were outlined with a black marking pen so that they could be seen more clearly in the photograph.

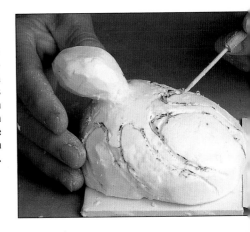

Use a shallow gouge to first outline the margins of the eight tentacles, and then remove the soap between them to make them stand out in relief form.

After slightly undercutting the margins of the tentacles, detail further as needed. The carving is then burnished with an abrasive pad.

After inserting red dressmaker's pins for eyes, the carving is further burnished by gently rubbing the carving with a damp plastic sponge.

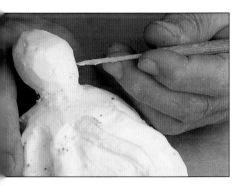

After tapering and rounding the surfaces of the tentacles, locate the eyes and outline them with a wooden needle.

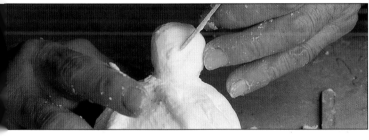

Elevate the eyes by removing soap from around the eye socket margins.

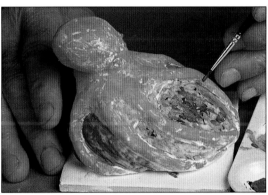

Brush a couple of coats of reddish-orange watercolor paint on the octopus. The rock is then painted a grayish shade with splashes of red and green added to represent algae and other biota growing on the rock.

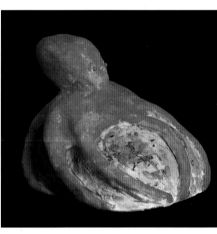

Oblique view of the painted Octopus

Groove behind the siphon to represent the anterior margin of the mantle.

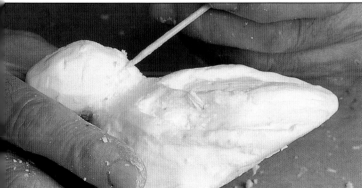

Outline tubular siphon. This is difficult to carve so you can represent it as a little bump. The alternative is to insert a small short plastic tube in the area. The problem is finding such an appropriately sized small tube. Medical intravenous polyethylene tubes would fit the bill, but are not readily available to the general public.

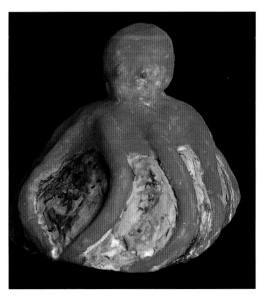

Frontal view of the painted Octopus

Chapter Fourteen
Templates

This chapter includes three blank templates that were used in this book. The templates are drawn and reproduced to the size of the bath size Ivory Soap® bar. The patterns have been included so that you can make copies of them and design your own carving patterns. You can, of course, create your own templates to fit the needs of your proposed soap carving designs.

Template for single bar of Ivory Soap®

Top, Lateral (side) view; bottom, Dorsal (top) view

Top, Ventral (abdominal) view; bottom, Frontal view.